Compositions: Janek Gwizdala
Design: Chelsea Gwizdala

VIDEO GUIDE

Use the following link to get free access to all video content for this book:

https://www.janeksbassstudio.com/courses/bass-player-s-guide-to-looping

BASS PLAYER'S GUIDE TO LOOPING

BY JANEK GWIZDALA

COPYRIGHT © 2019
BY JANEK GWIZDALA, LLC
ALL RIGHTS RESERVED

TO INFINITY & BEYOND

∞

TABLE OF CONTENTS

INTRODUCTION 6

REFERENCE
SIGNAL CHAIN 7
PEDAL SETTINGS 8

THE BASICS
HOW TO MAKE THE PERFECT LOOP 10
BE KIND TO YOUR AMP 10
PEDAL VOLUME 11

PRACTICE
BASIC PERCUSSIVE LOOP 12
MULTI-LAYERED PERCUSSIVE LOOP 13
JAMMING ON ONE CHORD 14
CHORD SEQUENCES 18
ii-V-I'S 20

COMPOSITION
RECORD YOUR SESSIONS 22
BASS LINE FIRST, MELODY SECOND 22
MELODY FIRST, BASS LINE SECOND 24
SONG FORM 25
MELODY HARMONIZATION 28
STACKING TRIADS 29

PERFORMANCE
LOW END 31
HIGH OSTINATO (REHARMONIZATION OPTIONS) 35
AMBIENT 37
SAMPLING USING A SECOND LOOPER 40
HOW MANY LAYERS TO ADD AT ONCE 41
LOOPING WITH A BAND/DRUMMER 43

CLOSING THOUGHTS 44

INTRODUCTION

Like a lot of things I've found joy in, live looping came about out of necessity. I find that when necessity is at the forefront, you tend to make things work with the tools you have. Along the way, you find ways in which to innovate, think outside the box, and find something new to explore.

I was at home in Los Angeles between projects, had a week open, and wanted to play a show somewhere. The where didn't matter. I simply needed someone to find a venue, some accommodation, and an audience, and then I would commit to buying a plane ticket and going anywhere in the world to perform solo. Thanks to Julian and Frankie and the whole crew in Costa Rica, this idea would become the very first show of my completely solo "Last-Minute World Tour" in the end of 2016.

I literally arrived to the show having no idea what I was going to play, or how I was going to play it. I had two loop pedals with me, if I remember correctly; a few other effects, and my bass. That's it. I remember thinking to myself, "If I can make it to 45 minutes, then I'm in pretty good shape. I'll take a few questions from the audience, and I'll be able to string out one last song to make it to one hour."

When the show was reaching 90 minutes and the audience was still completely engaged, and I was still coming up with ideas to play, I had a feeling I might be onto something—maybe this wouldn't just be a one-off show. This concept ended up taking me all over the world, and I visited more than 50 cities on the 2016-2017 Last-Minute World Tour.

Something I would like to be very specific about before we get going is that everything contained in this book—while it could well apply conceptually to a multitude of looping setups—is coming from a stomp-box/pedal standpoint. I'm not a specialist when it comes to midi triggering, Ableton Live, computers, backing tracks, rack-mounted gear, or any other looping wizardry. My main touring rig consists of 8 stomp boxes plus a volume pedal (which all fit into a small camera bag), and they are all I need to create a compelling 90+ minute show as a solo artist. So, when looping tools are mentioned in this book, that's the angle we're coming from.

You also don't need to own or use any of the pedals I talk about in this book (besides the obvious looper) to make use of all the concepts. A volume pedal can be substituted with the volume knob on your bass, and the vast majority of the other effects we talk about with pedals can be recreated in some way or another using just the bass.

Now that you know where I'm coming from, and how I managed to create a completely solo show based around looping with a pedal, let's go through all the ways that I use this pedal, and how it can help you become a much better musician. There are limitless directions you can explore with this tool, and all of them will help you on your path to becoming a more creative, honest, and artistic master of your musical voice and your instrument.

Janek

REFERENCE:
SIGNAL CHAIN & PEDAL SETTINGS

I set up my pedals in a rather non-traditional manner, in that I don't use a pedal board. I place them in a straight line in front of me, with the signal running from right to left. I also sit when I play, making it easier to lean forward and manipulate pedal settings during a performance.

The key with the loop pedal (or pedals) is that they need to be positioned at the very end of the signal chain. This gives you the ability to record anything that's happening with any other pedal in the setup, which requires that the loopers go last.

My volume pedal is always up front, so I can manipulate the input gain into any of the pedals in the chain. This is followed closely by my Miura M2 compressor, the Boss OC2 octave pedal, the Boss PS5 Super Shifter, the Fredric Effects Bug Crusher, TC Electronic's Hall Of Fame Reverb, and finally TC Electronic's Nova Repeater delay, before getting to our target of the looper.

As I mentioned before, you do not need these exact pedals to employ all the concepts in this book; only the looping pedal of your choice. This is just my particular setup, and this is what I'll be referring to throughout the book.

SIGNAL CHAIN: RIGHT TO LEFT

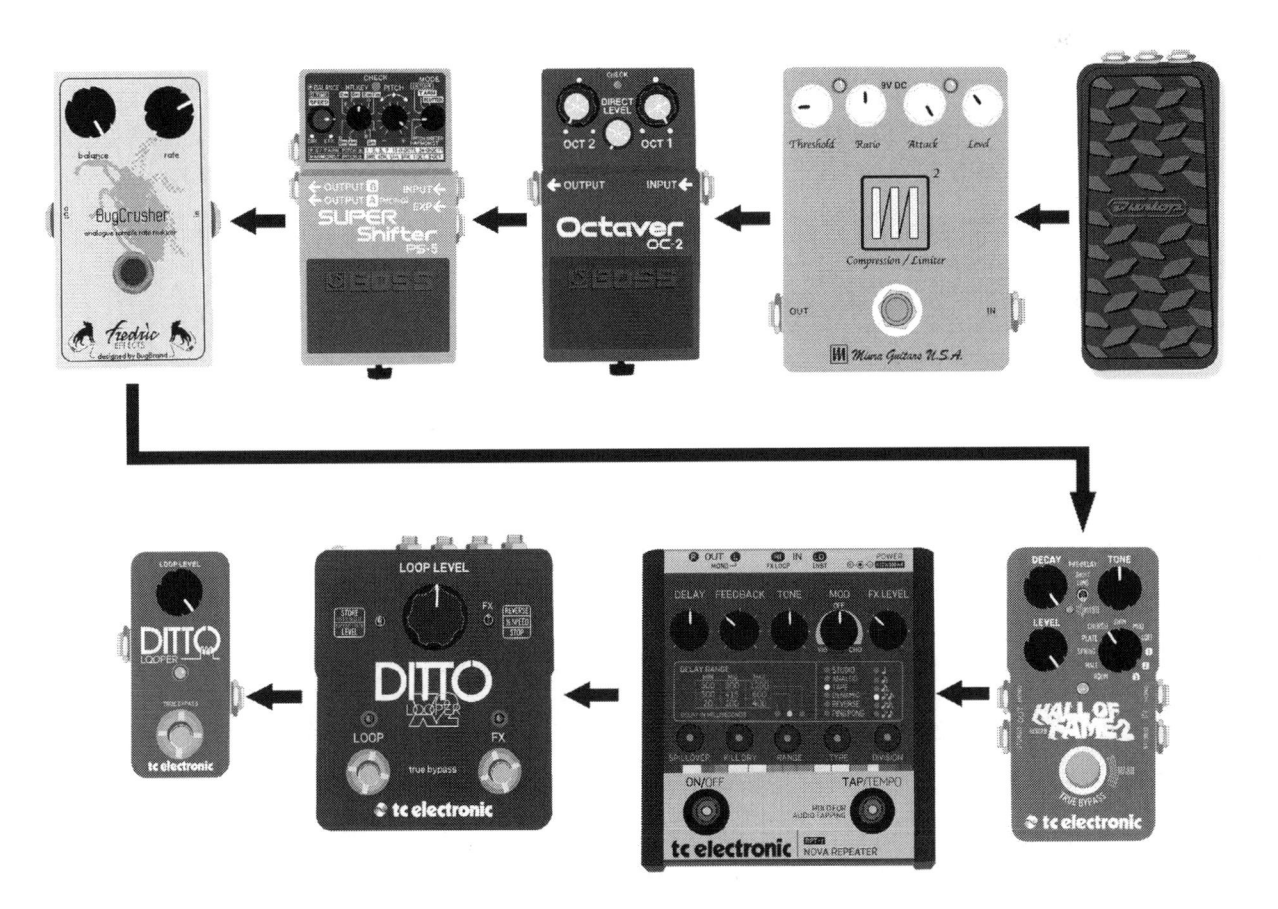

PEDAL SETTINGS

Dunlop Volume Pedal

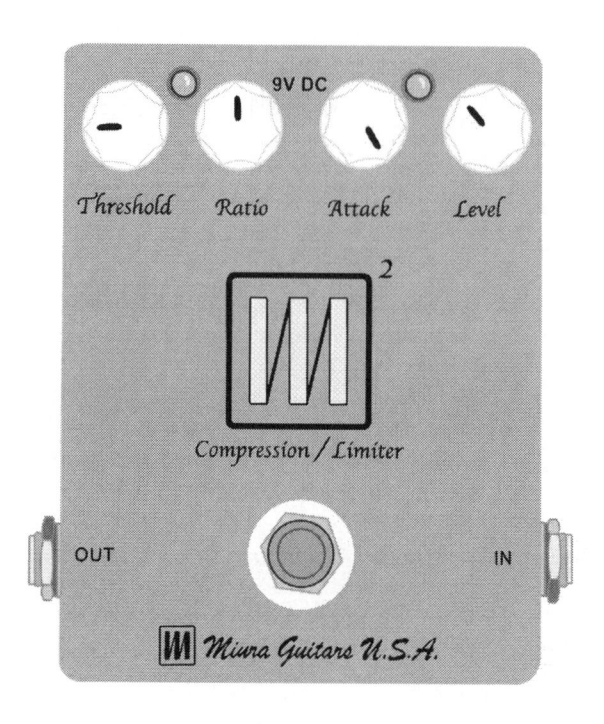

Miura Compressor

Boss Super Shifter PS-5

Boss Octaver OC-2

**Fredric Effects
BugCrusher**
(Bit Crusher)

**TC Electronic
Hall of Fame 2**
(Reverb)

**TC Electronic
Mini Ditto Looper**

**TC Electronic
Nova Repeater**
(Delay)

**TC Electronic
Ditto Looper X2**

THE BASICS

1) How to Make the Perfect Loop

There is, of course, no shortcut around simply having good time. But timing the repeat of the loop can often be the most challenging part of the entire looping process. Just like anything else, it takes plenty of practice to be calm while you do this.

One of the easiest ways I've found to make sure you achieve a perfect loop every time is to play through the downbeat as you hit the loop button. Your goal is to avoid the momentary disconnect between what you're playing with your hands, and what is going on with your foot and the pedal. By doing both at the same time, you won't be transferring your focus too heavily from one thing to the other, and it will be a far more natural transition.

2) Be Kind to your Amp

Don't overload the looper too early on in your setup, especially if you plan to have many ideas stacked on top of each other. Remember that, for the most part, you're going to be pushing all of these layers in your loop into a bass amp. That amp is typically only dealing with whatever you can play at one time, not with 20+ versions of you. Being aware of the volume level in those establishing layers of a loop performance will pay off big time in terms of your sound quality as the loop builds.

3) Pedal Volume

Check to be sure where the "zero-decibel" level sits on the volume knob of your loop pedal (in other words, the level setting that neither increases or decreases the natural volume of the signal chain). If your loop pedal is unintentionally set at zero *volume* instead of zero *decibles*, or anywhere far below the volume of your signal chain, your latest and greatest creation will seem to have vanished after hitting the repeat button. (Yes, that has absolutely happened to me on huge live shows, and I've been sitting there staring sheepishly at my loop pedal with the volume at zero. Not a great look, and not a great feeling either.)

Get in the habit of cleaning out previous loops from your pedal, and check that the volume is at zero decibles each time you finish with it. This will help to ensure you never run into the silence-on-stage issue.

	Correct Setting (Zero DB)	**Incorrect Setting**
Ditto X2	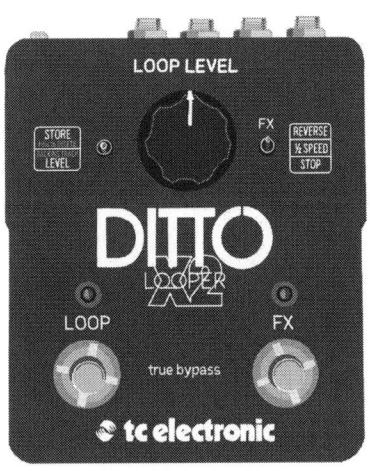 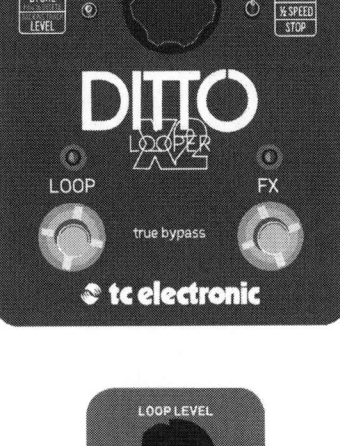	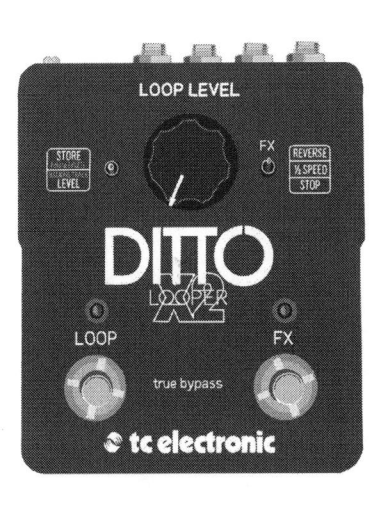
Ditto Mini Looper		

PRACTICE

The loop pedal is, without a doubt, my most valuable practice tool. The options are endless, and this chapter will highlight some of my favorite concepts for populating your practice routine.

1) Basic Percussive Loop

Using your left (or fretting) hand to mute the strings, use the low string on your bass (E or B) to mimic a kick drum, and then a higher string to take the place of a snare drum (picking the kick-drum sound with the thumb, and the snare sound with the middle finger).

I don't automatically pick the lowest and the highest strings on the bass to create these drum sounds, and the tone of both these percussive elements will depend on a number of factors:

1) if your bass is running clean (no effects)
2) the position of your muting hand on the neck of the instrument
3) the three main variants of plucking the strings: Slap/Thumb, Palm Muted, or Open.

Experimenting with all of these options is key when building your vocabulary with this style of looping.

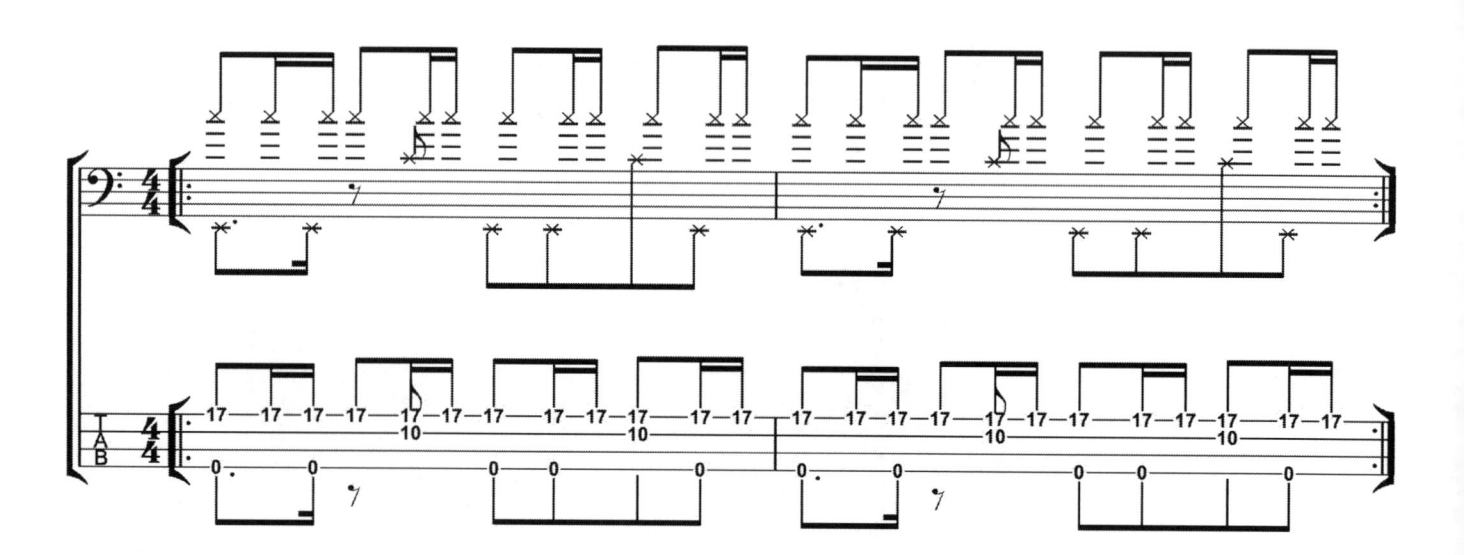

2) Multi-Layered Percussive Loop

Taking all of the options in the "Basic Percussive Loop" example, I want to look at layering other percussive elements into your virtual drum set, and give you some concepts of mimicking a broad range of sounds with the bass. I love to use the Boss PS5 Super-Shifter with the octave-up, and double octave-up functions, for really high-pitched percussion. I'm hearing things like shakers, hi-hats, triangles, tambourines, and any small percussion instrument you might find in a pro percussionist's setup onstage.

I would recommend starting out simple, and using a dry sound (with no reverb or delay), to work on creating a high pitched pulse that could take the role of the hi-hat in a drum set. You do not need the Boss PS5 to accomplish this specifically, but you will have to get more creative with your muting on the neck of the instrument to produce higher-pitched percussive notes.

I've also achieved these effects by tapping the pickups with a metallic object, using a guitar pick or a coin to scrape the strings (if you're using round wounds), or literally picking up objects around me onstage and experimenting with them on the instrument—all in search of new weird and wonderful percussive sounds.

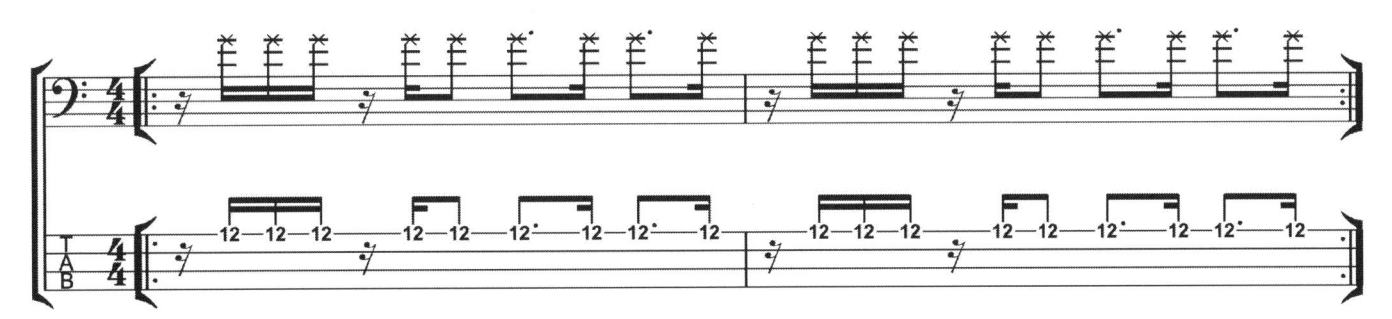

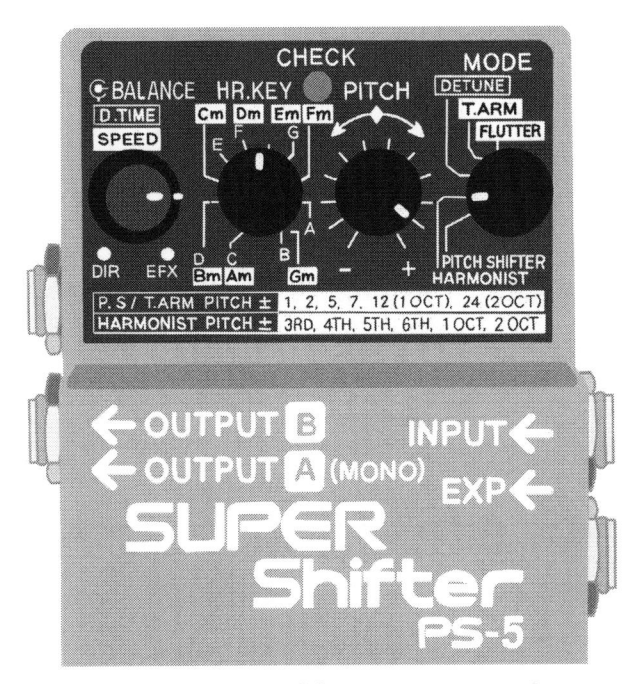

Boss PS-5: Double-Octave Setting
(Pitch Wheel to Penultimate Notch)

Boss PS-5: Triple-Octave Setting
(Pitch Wheel to Final Notch)

The next thing to try is to use the same high-pitched tones, but adding a little delay. When you're playing "dry," you have to manually pick every single note and element you want in your loop. But with a delay, there are a myriad of options. This allows you to do far less picking with your right hand, and let the pedal do a lot of the rhythmic work. I also like the fact that there will be some decay with the sound, which adds to the shape and organic nature of the effect.

One of the most common rhythms in delay pedals is often a dotted-note value. Whether that's an 8th note or a whole note, be sure to use the tap tempo on the pedal to tap along with the tempo of the loop. Then experiment with very sparse attacks with your picking hand, letting the delay do most of the work for you.

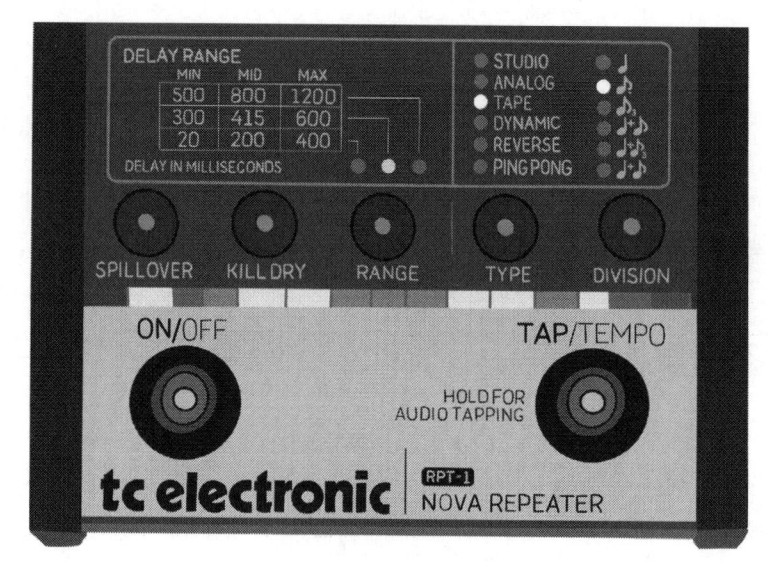

**Nova Repeater:
Dotted-Eighth Setting**

3) Jamming on One Chord

When it comes to getting started with harmony and melody in the loop pedal, there might not be an easier place to begin than setting up a one-chord jam. This can start with a bass line, and then be expanded with any or all of the percussive concepts we just talked about. I love to keep this stuff SIMPLE! The last thing I want to do is commit to something in the looper that is super busy. The busier the initial loop, the less space you'll have to grow what you're working on.

In terms of the layers of this one-chord jam, there are a few ways to approach it. You can start off with a bass line, add some percussion, and away you go soloing on top of the loop. You can also flip the process in terms of the harmony: start out with a chord, add some percussion, and then choose whether you go straight to working on melodic content on top of that, or whether you add a bass line to your chord. There's no "correct" way to do it; simply be aware of the huge range of options available to you.

One-Chord Jam: Chords First

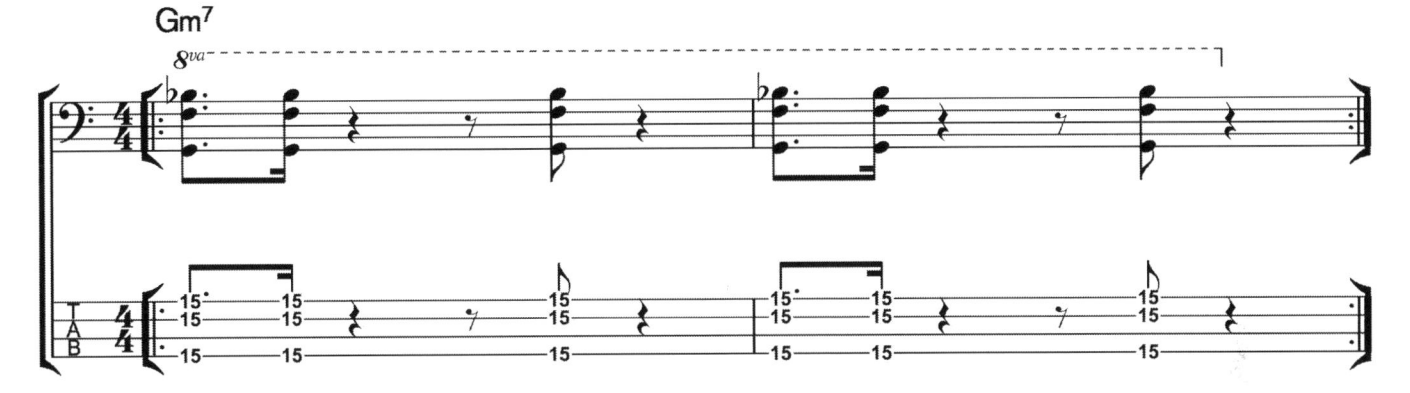

One-Chord Jam: Adding a Bass Line

If I have a new phrase I'm trying to add to my vocabulary, a one-chord loop is the perfect place to be able to play that phrase over and over again in as close to a real-life musical performance situation as possible.

One-Chord Jam: Practicing a Phrase

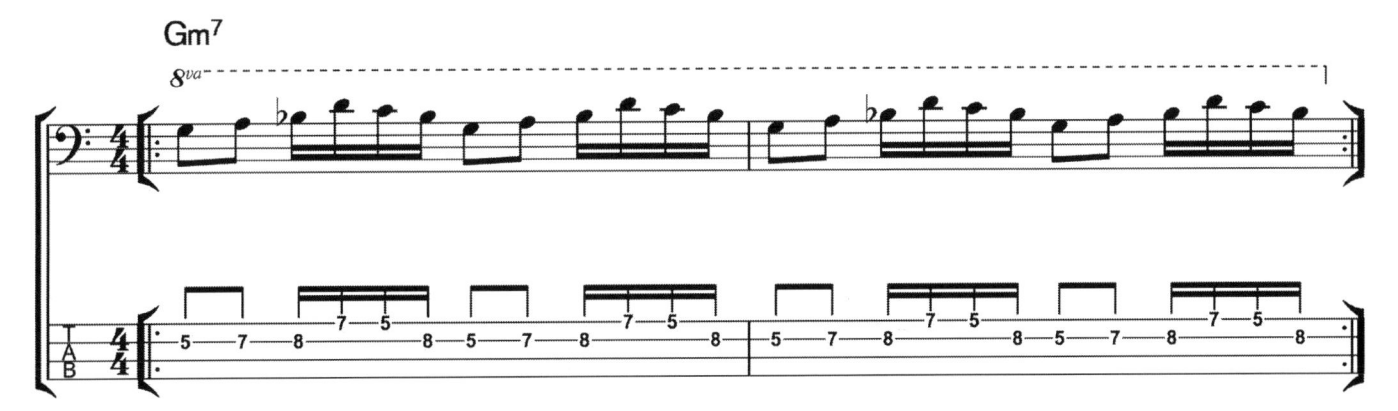

Another use of the one-chord jam, which I've found priceless in my practice routine over the years, is the ability to experiment with playing outside the changes. You can discover how a certain phrase feels completely inside the key center, then move it around the neck—either randomly, or in some form of intervalic sequence (i.e. in half steps/whole steps/minor thirds). Finally, go in search of all the places you can resolve back into the key center. The art of creating and releasing tension in this way is one of the biggest building blocks of jazz improvisation. It helps create a picture, a story, and a conversation when you play, and the loop pedal has been my biggest ally when working on this style of playing.

Be sure to experiment with the differences between playing outside over a bass line (which is usually inherently sparse and open), and playing outside over three- or four-note chord voicings which might dictate the harmony a little more (not only because they are more dense, but because they might also be in a similar register to your melodic content).

One-Chord Jam: Moving a Phrase in Half-Steps

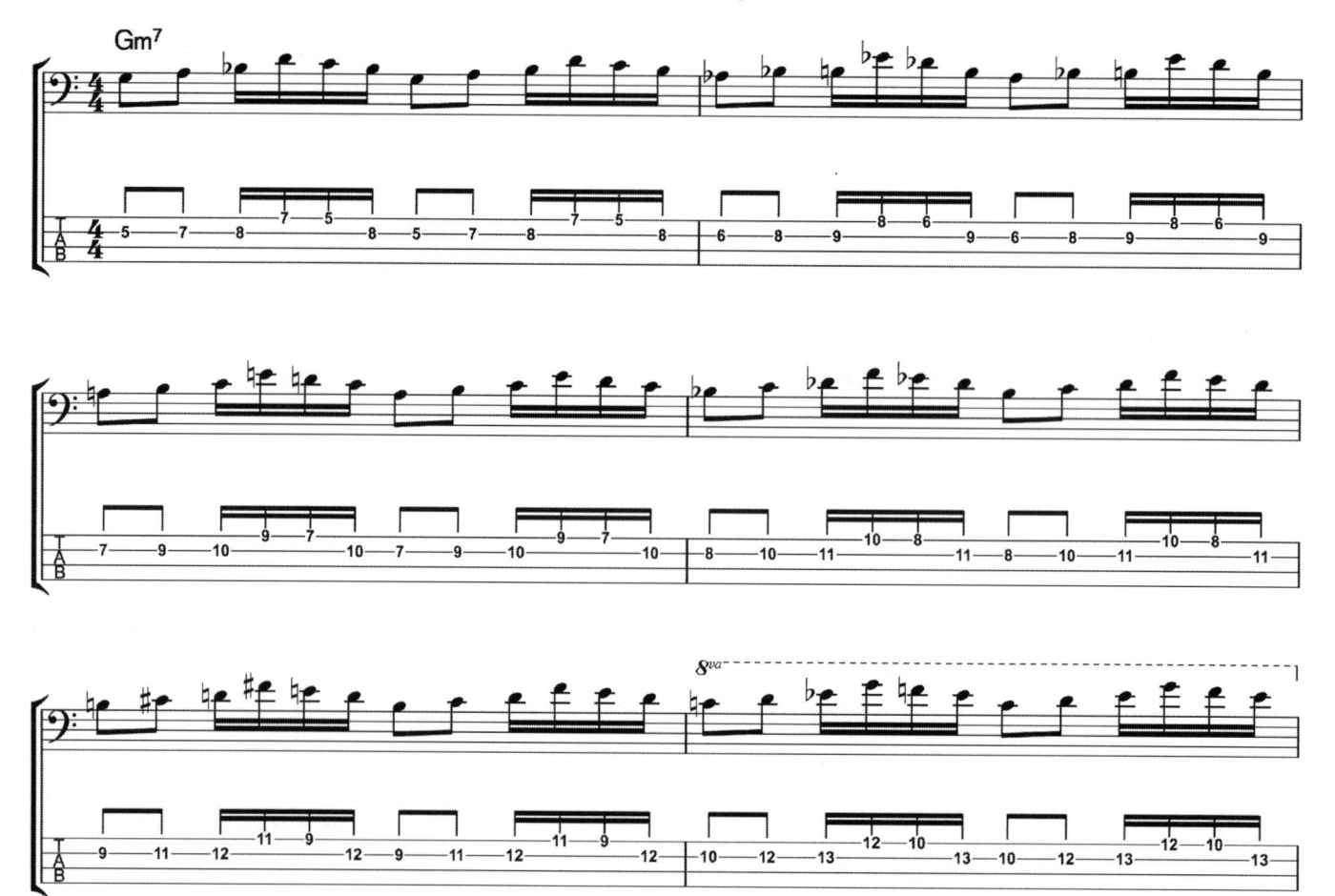

One-Chord Jam: Moving a Phrase in Whole-Steps

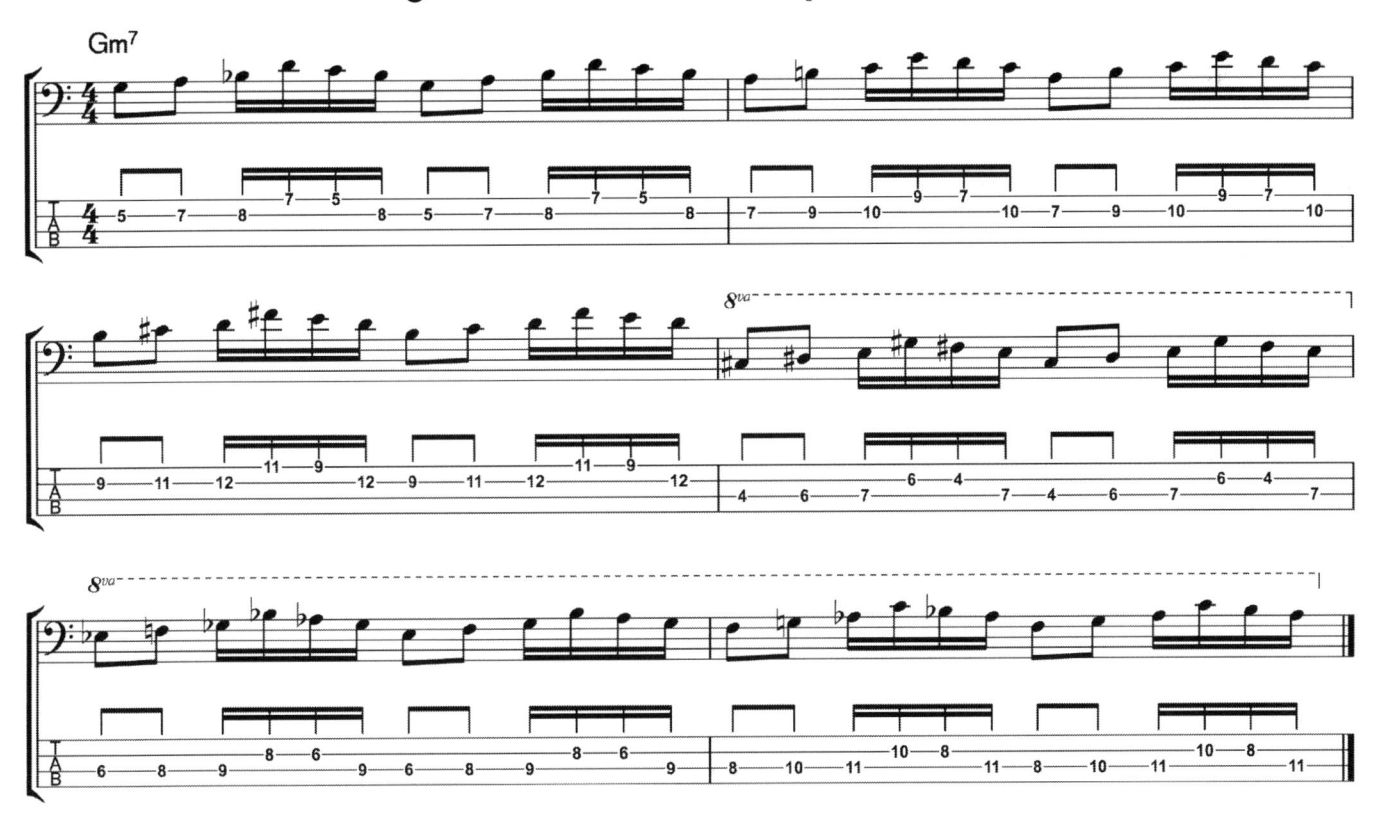

One-Chord Jam: Moving a Phrase in Minor Thirds

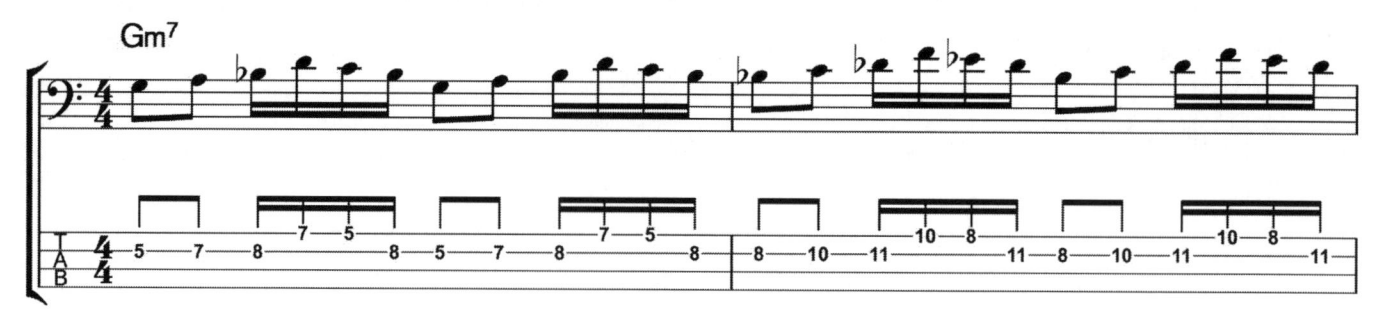

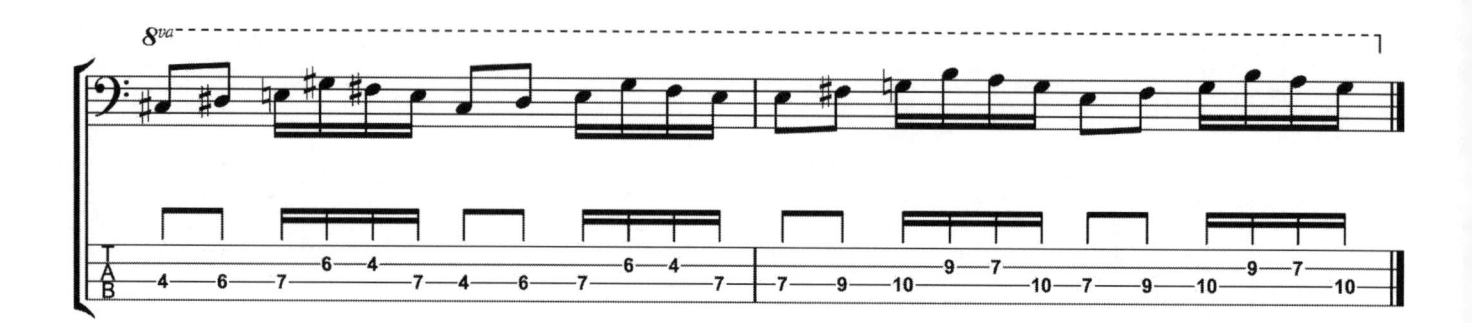

4) Chord Sequences

A natural progression from the one-chord jam is to expand the harmonic rhythm, and work on your consistency in being able to play things in all twelve keys. Take the same chord quality from your one-chord jam, for example, and pick three other key centers; then play those with your original chord, to create a four-chord sequence.

The same applies for moving a shape around the instrument—but this time, we're trying to make a smooth transition through our four new chords. There are many factors that will influence this concept, including tempo, length of your melodic phrase, and harmonic rhythm of your changes. Do you have one chord per bar? Two? Maybe even four? How many times can you play the phrase over one chord? Is the phrase short, and easy to move between each chord? Or is it an odd number of notes? And does it cross the bar line?

If you're having any issues with the fluidity of your practice routine, don't be afraid to simplify—strip back the number of components in your exercises, and take away notes until you're 100% comfortable with a phrase. Then, add in the elements that were giving you trouble one at a time. Look back on this list of possible scenarios and see which, if any, might be applicable to your current situation.

Awareness of your routine and your process, and of the building blocks that create them, is the absolute key to improving not just your playing, but the way in which you develop your ideas.

Four-Chord Sequence Example

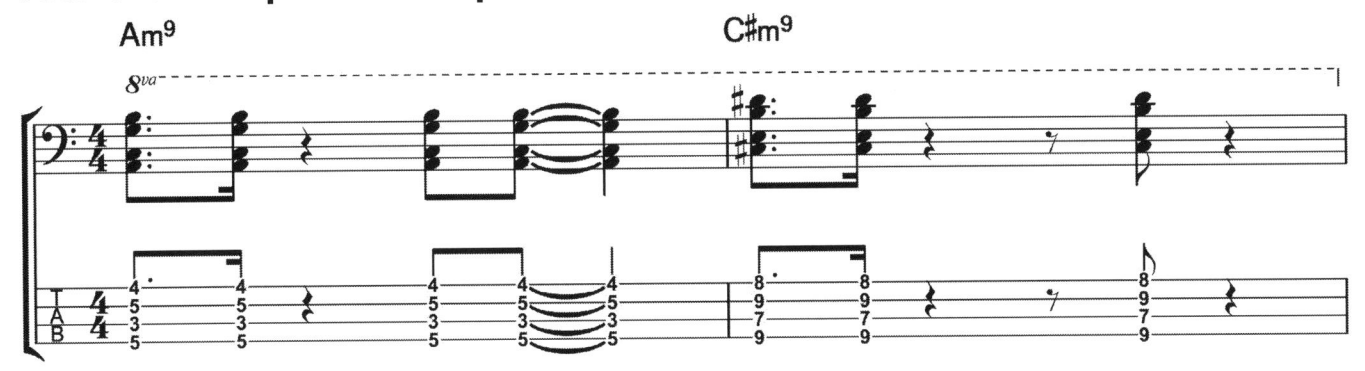

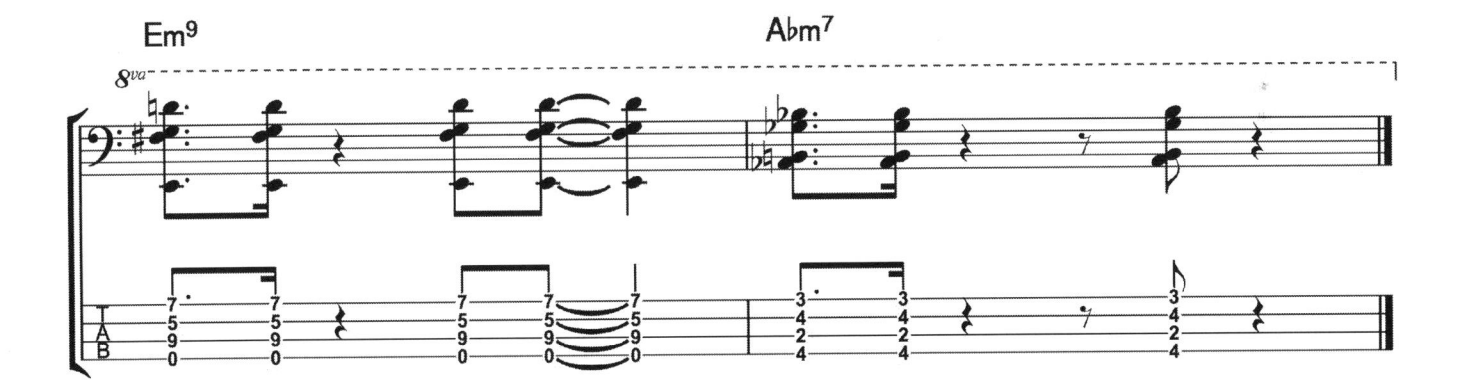

Four-Chord Sequence Example: Melodic Phrase

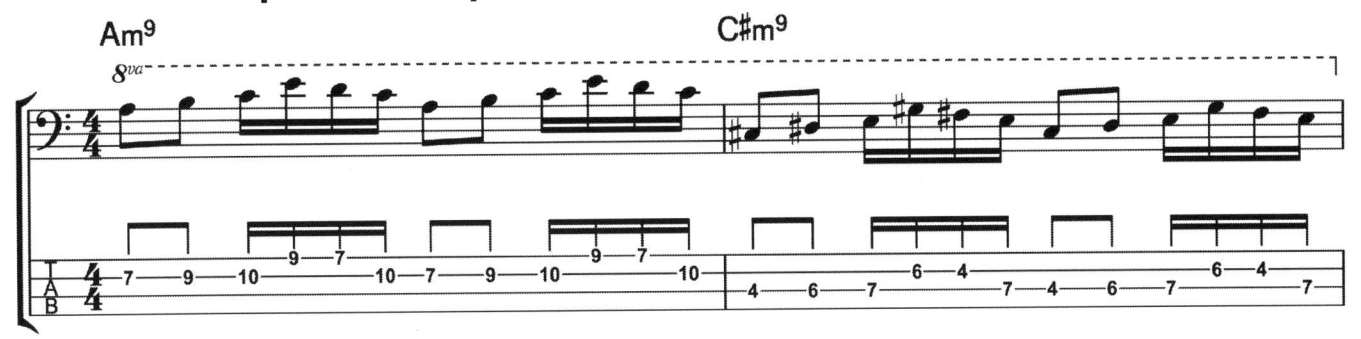

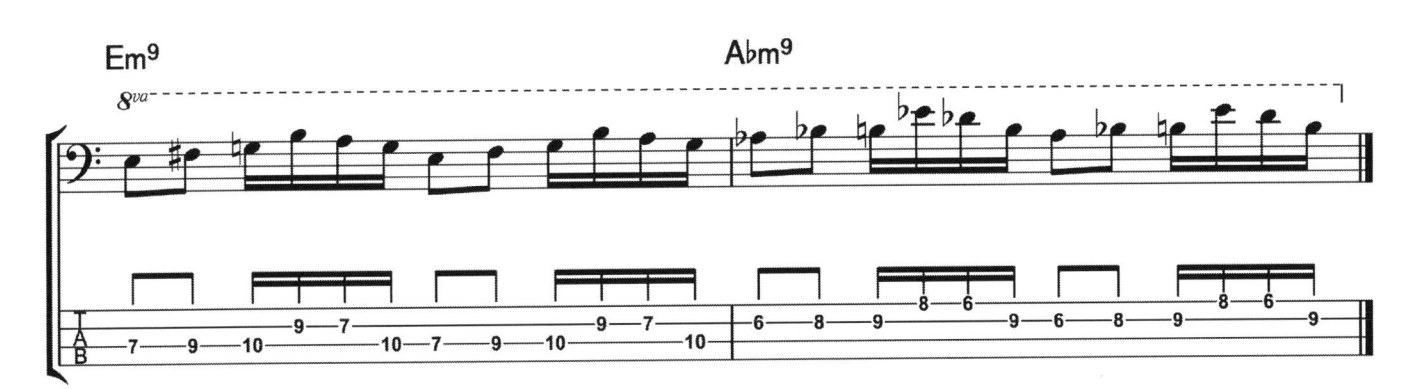

5) ii-V-I

This wouldn't be a Janek Gwizdala practice chapter without adding some ideas for ii-V-I vocabulary-building using the looper. From a ii-V-I in one key, to adding the VI, to putting complete song forms of standards into the looper, I've tried it all, and it's all helpful to your playing.

Playing the entire form of a jazz standard into the looper is a great way to work on your time, and to receive some immediate feedback on the consistency of your tempo when you get back to the top of the form. It's easy to complete the form of the song in the looper and instantly hear that your tempo is either slightly faster or slower at the end of the form than the beginning. This is a great exercise for focus and concentration. It can be very easy to space out during a song form—especially if it's long, like "Lush Life" or "Moments Notice," or if it contains a lot of complex chord changes. But the looper is the ultimate judge of your time, and never lies to you—you get out of it exactly what you put in.

Although I rarely find myself playing walking bass lines in a jazz context (as an electric bass player), that feel is still one of my favorites to practice over. As a result, it will often be my go-to time feel when I'm working on jazz vocabulary in the looper (such as ii-V-I's). I like to add a back beat into the looper (on beats two & four), as a drummer might with their cross-stick on the snare.

ii-V-I Walking Bass Line Example

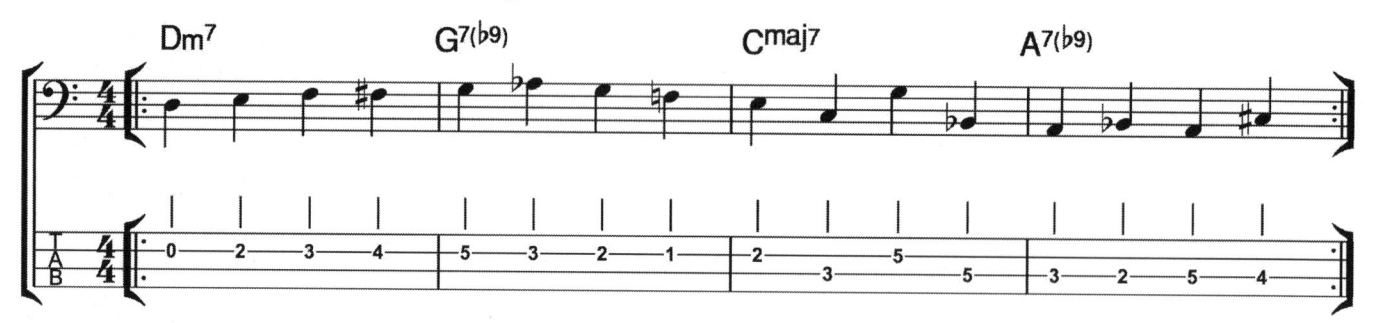

ii-V-I Phrase Example

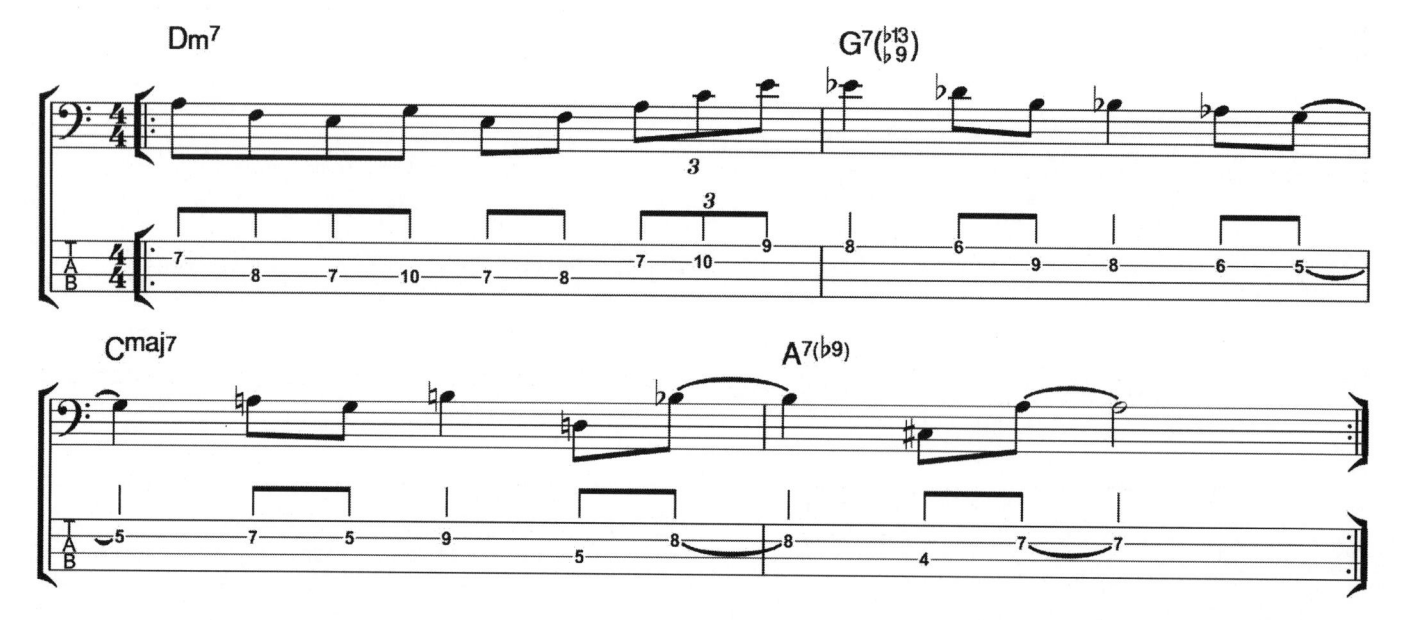

When I have a significant chunk of time to work on this material, I'll often put ii-V-I's in the looper in multiple keys, and work on my discipline of being able to take one phrase seamlessly through that sequence. Again, your consistency of time will be highlighted here: with four bars per ii-V-I in six different keys, you're looking at a 24-bar form (with a lot of time passing from the beginning to the end, at a medium tempo). Being able to nail that loop at the exact same tempo you started it is not only essential, but super satisfying as well. Eventually, with enough time spent working on it, the time will become completely intuitive, buried in your subconscious and muscle memory.

COMPOSITION

So many of my compositions have emerged from jamming for hours and hours over a bass line. I find that the more time I spend with a groove, the greater likelihood that I'll run out of predictable stuff to play over it; out of necessity, I come up with things I've never played before.

To me, this is "the zone." This is the part of my practice/composition time where the most ideas come to life. How long it takes to get there and the amount of time it lasts in each session may vary, but simply being aware that it could be right around the corner can really dial in the intent with which you work. I think of it as being methodical in my intent, but spontaneous as the same time; never sacrificing creativity for routine, but always giving myself the best foundation for success by being aware of the fundamentals.

1) Record your Practice Sessions

Regardless of your conceptual approach to composition, I cannot highlight enough the importance of recording your practice sessions. It can be infuriating to jam along to a loop looking for melodic ideas, play something worth remembering only once, but then have no way to return to it once it slips from your memory.

It's a matter of being disciplined to automatically go for your voice recorder, or hit record if you're wired into your home studio. The more you can categorize and label your recordings, the better— even if it's just a key signature, time signature, and date. Find your own way of making sure you can get some use out of these recordings at a later date, and stick to it.

2) Bass Line First, Melody Second

Recording a bass line into the looper first gives us a great foundation upon which to build our melodic content. Listening to a consistent form allows freedom to experiment with space, just as much as you might experiment with linear ideas.

When writing melodies, the tendency can often be to rely on density, creating phrases that are too verbose. My goal is always to say us much as I can with as few notes as possible, and the space provided by a looped bass line allows me to arrive at that balance of brevity and impact almost immediately.

Bass Line First:

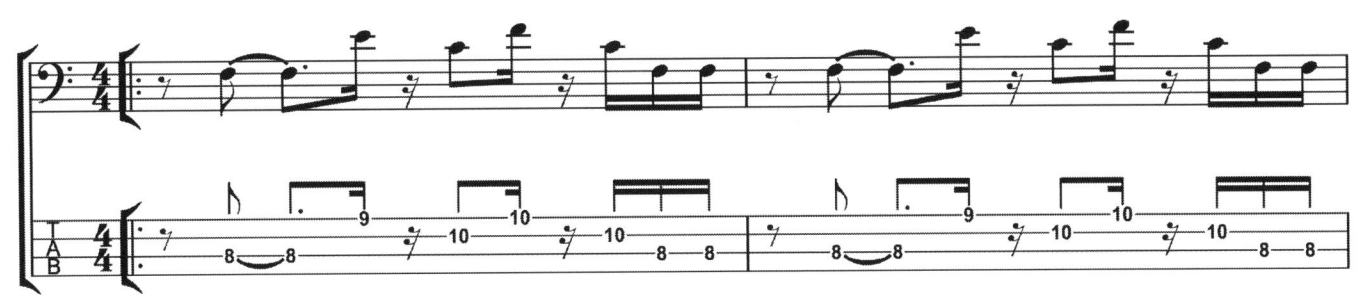

Melody Second:

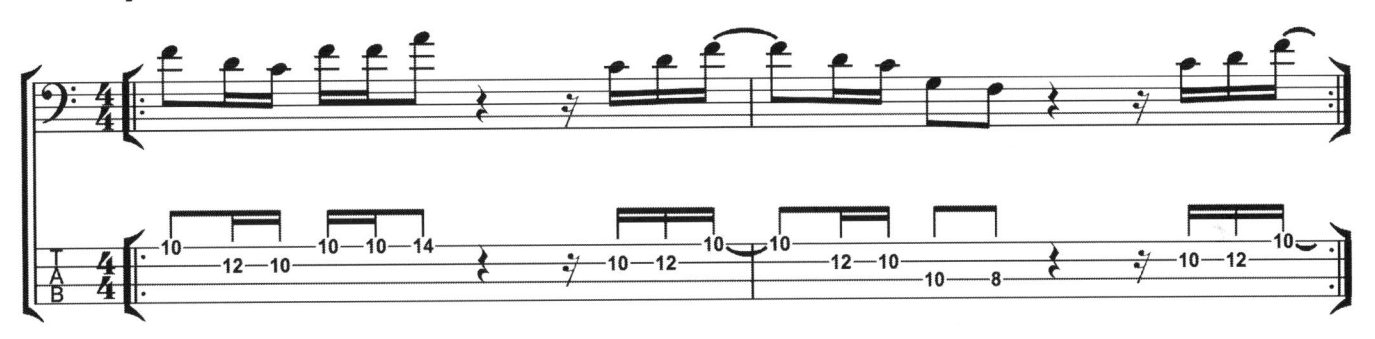

"To Begin" is a good example of something incredibly basic that ended up flourishing into the opening track of "The Space In Between." From two chords came a quirky bass line, and a simple melody—but when harmonized and played by incredible musicians, it took on new life and direction.

No matter how simple or "throw-away" you think it might be, don't discount an idea. Record it, label it, and archive it. When you're able to scroll through tons of your own ideas for compositions, you'll be glad you did.

"To Begin" by Janek Gwizdala

Cm7

Gm7

Cm7

Gm7

3) Melody First, Bass Line Second

Coming at the process from the opposite direction means you have the potential melody to a song before anything else. Once it's in the looper, you can search for possible harmony options underneath.

Beginning with the melody brings up a whole new set of technical obstacles with the looper: it won't always start on the downbeat of the bar. You might not be as used to hitting the loop button on the "and" of beat three, for instance, if that's where your melody starts.

A quick fix for this is to go back to our very first starting point for a loop, and put a percussive track into the looper first. That way, the framework for the song section is set, and you can add the melody to it with ease.

I do recommend practicing the loop entry either way, and being able to literally start with just the melody and nothing else. This will increase your comfort level with the pedal overall, and give you far more options if you ever perform these ideas live.

Melody First:

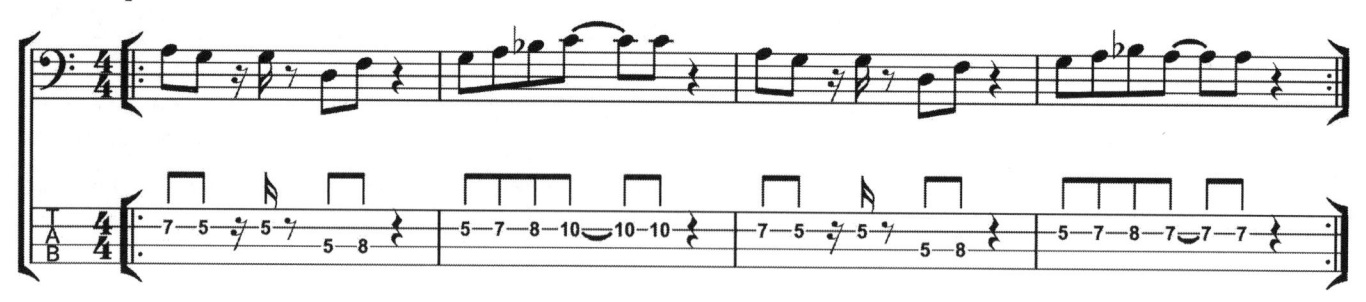

Bass Line Second:

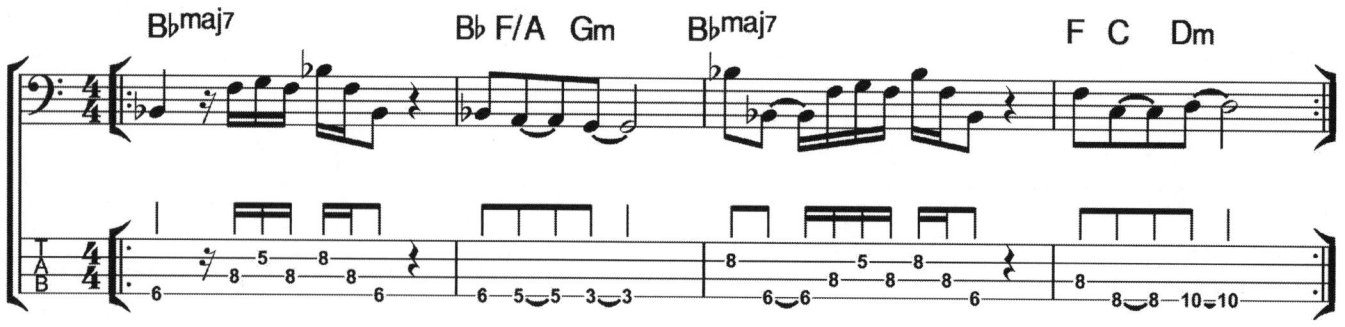

4) Song Form

My journey with loop pedals started out with the old Line6 DL4. You might have seen it in a museum: a big, cumbersome, green box with four buttons. I think it allowed for a maximum of 14 seconds of continuous record time (28 seconds if you hit the half-speed button before recording). It didn't do much for long-form or through-composed music. It did sound amazing, and I can say nothing but good things about the time I spent with it, but technology has advanced considerably since then. My current collection of Ditto loopers all have around 5 minutes of record time.

To reiterate the importance of recording my practice sessions: I'm generally working on one small section of a song at a time. That involves a ton of repetition, refining the melody, looking for the best root motions, and generally dialing in the song section as much as possible before moving on. It's not until I've done that with at least two sections—maybe a verse and a chorus—that I'll attempt to put both of those sections in the looper, so I can start cycling a large part of a composition. Only then will I get a feel for what it might need next.

Again, we face the challenge of metronomic consistency here—like inputing the entire form of a jazz standard. There's also the task of remembering all the components of your composition so far.

It can be very helpful to work on this stage of the composition for a long period of time, if you ever plan to use the looper for a live solo performance. The more relaxed you are with your own music, and all the layers of each song, the better. It's a common issue to be so caught up in the organizing, booking, traveling to, and setting up for a gig, that we often overlook the need to actually practice our own music. Therefore, the constant repetition of playing song forms into the looper when you have the luxury of a no-pressure home environment has a huge payoff down the line.

You might also want to think about the form of your loop as being vertical, rather than horizontal. Once you've locked in a loop, you can work on a slow dynamic build, adding elements to your loop as markers of a vertical form. I've created loops that weren't necessarily the longest forms you've ever heard—sometimes just eight bars—but I was able to create form and interest in the performance by being very compositional with layers. What starts out as a calm, ambient drone could well turn into a six-part harmony, with huge bass drops and a virtual percussion ensemble. More on that in the performance chapter of this book later.

We'll use my song "Erdnase" as an example of having a complete song form to work with in the looper. I wrote the song exactly as I described above: I first spent time looping just the "A" and "B" sections separately, solidifying them in my muscle memory, before working on looping the entire "AAB" form of the song.

Song Form Example:
"Erdnase" by Janek Gwizdala

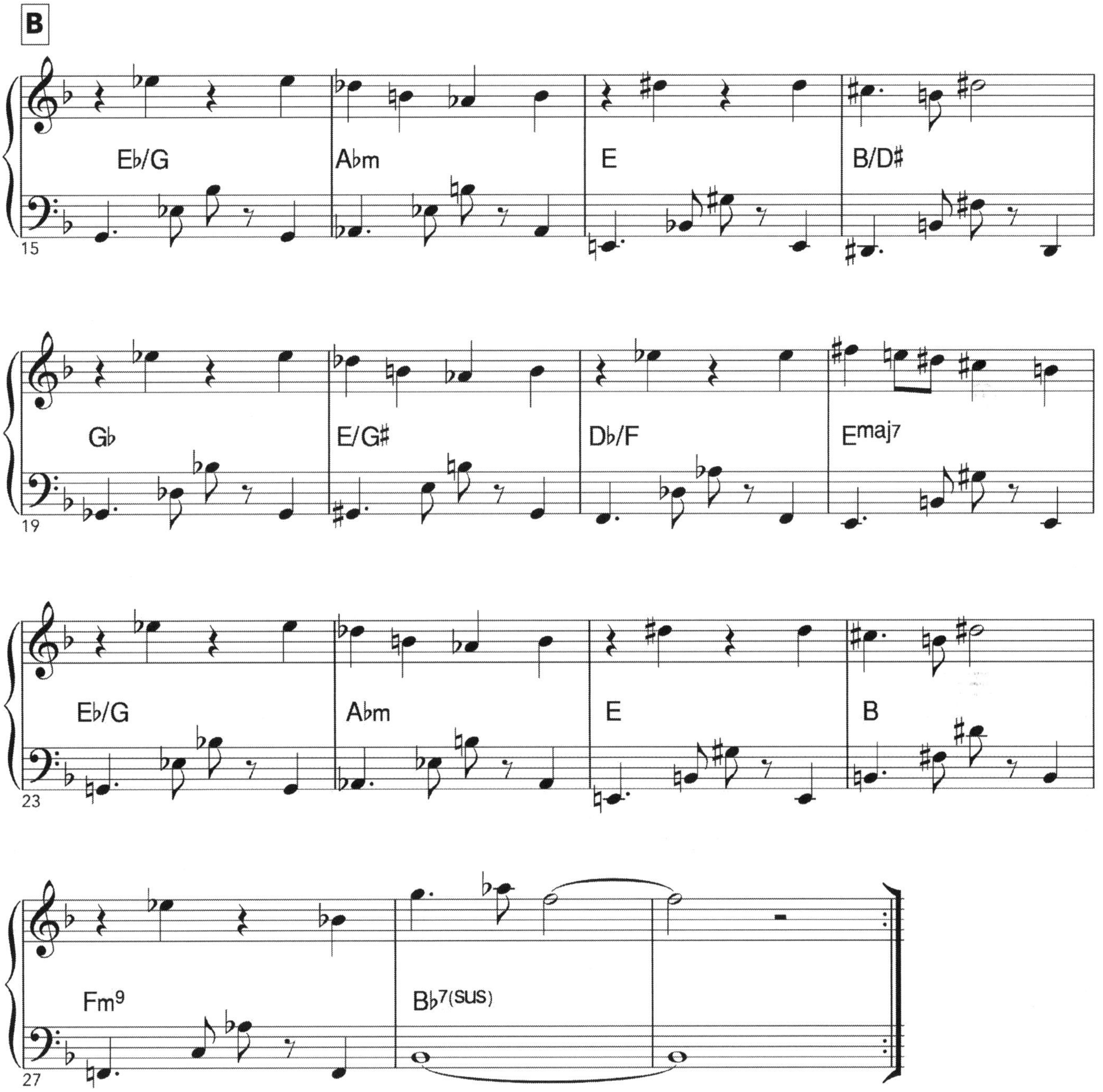
B
E♭/G
A♭m
E
B/D♯
15
G♭
E/G♯
D♭/F
Emaj7
19
E♭/G
A♭m
E
B
23
Fm9
B♭7(sus)
27

5) Melody Harmonization

Whether you're a wiz at harmonization of melodies or you're completely new to it, the loop pedal is an amazing facilitator of exploration and trial & error. I love coming up with a melody over a set of chord changes I have in the looper, and then trying to find the perfect harmony notes to give it that wow-factor.

Here's the best part about it: You don't have to have an advanced degree in music theory to make any of this happen. If you have zero music-theory knowledge, you simply have to be open to working on this technique through trial and error, until you come up with a set of harmonic options that can be worked into your muscle memory through repetition.

I got most of my intuition about harmonizing melodies from great singers, without even realizing it. I would hear that moment where the background vocals kick in behind a lead singer, and get goose bumps from the way the notes blended together. When it came time to explore that for myself in my own playing, I had this built-in sense memory. With trial and error, as well as training my ear, it didn't take long to work out that—more often than not—the harmony is actually quite elementary. The intervals of a third and a sixth will definitely be your friend when practicing this, and it's just a matter of time before the "right" harmony notes become a natural extension of your playing.

When I implore you to start simple with this (if you don't have much experience of harmonizing a melody), I truly mean *simple*. A major or minor chord, a diatonic melody, and just thirds or sixths are more than enough material to begin.

Melody Harmonization Example: Bass Line

Melody Harmonization Example: Melody

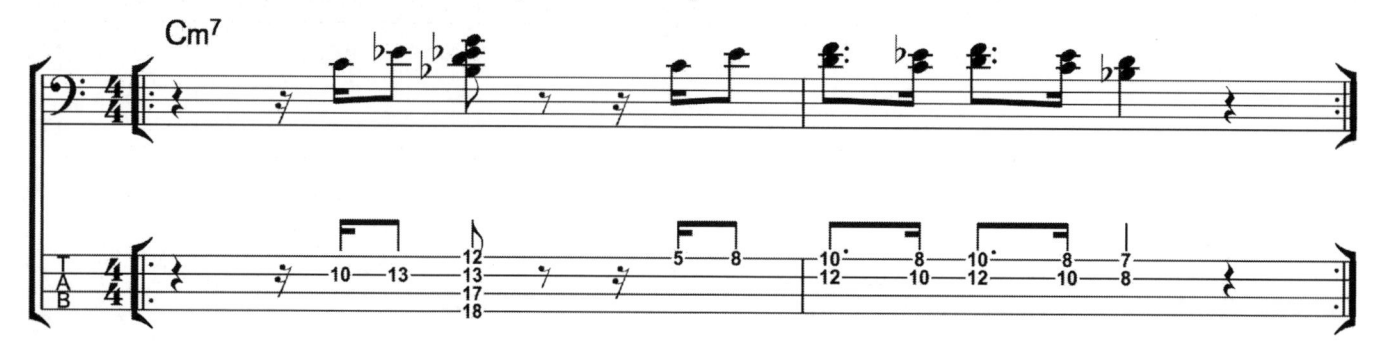

If your goal with any of this is solo performance, you will need to experiment with the range of your instrument, and figure out where certain intervals work the best. That's true for all the elements we've talked about, but is especially true for a melody. The melody is most likely what people are going to walk away remembering from your performance, so it's key to serve that melody as best you can, and not bury it with an overwhelming amount of harmonies and comping. Simple is always more effective. Your melody has to be strong, but effective orchestration of that melody is almost always what helps your audience to remember it.

6) Stacking Triads

Stacking triads is something I've heard so many piano players do over the years, and in this example I'm really channeling Russell Ferrante of the Yellowjackets. It's so much a part of his sound when he's comping, and when he's arranging harmony for his music—and I didn't realize how much you could emulate that with a looper until I started tracking just a few notes at a time. It's impossible to voice all six notes of two stacked triads at once on the bass—but when layering them with the looper, you can create these amazingly lush beds of harmony, widening your sound and harmonic palette in a big way.

Stacking Triads Example: Lower Set

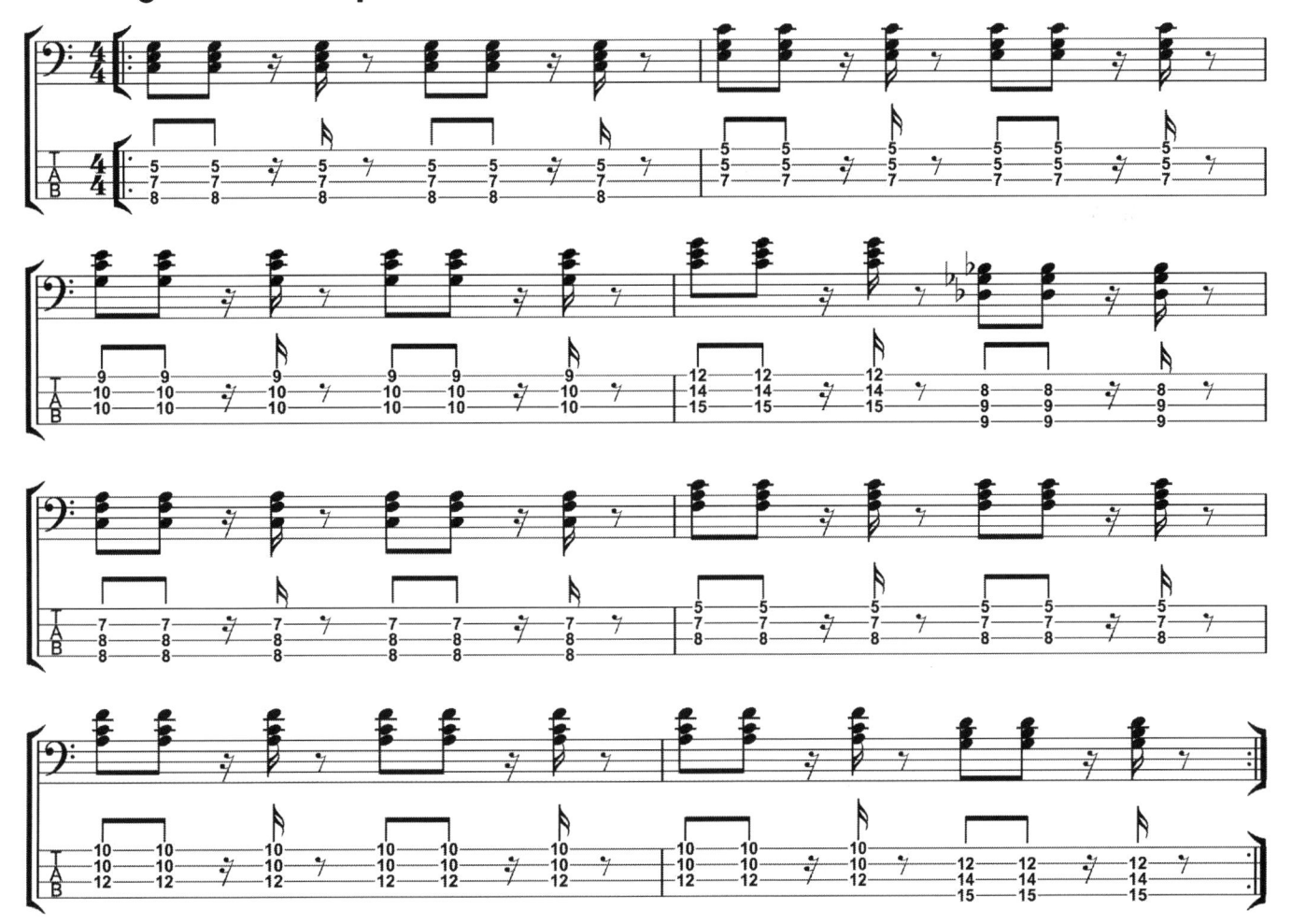

Stacking Triads Example: Upper Set

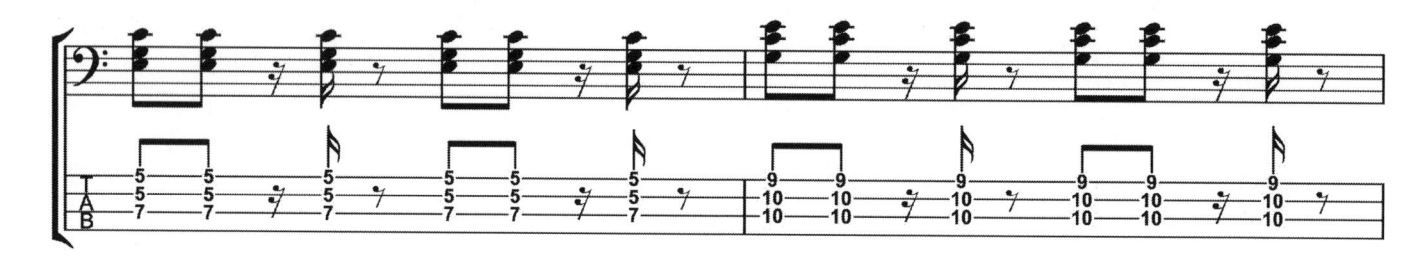

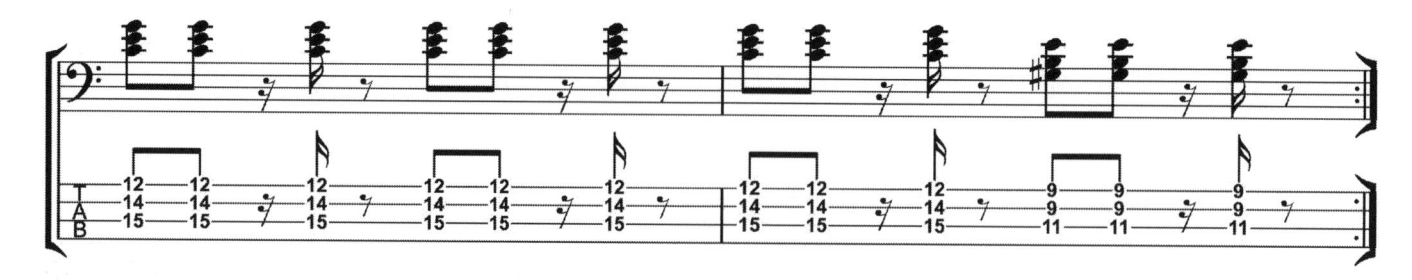

Stacking Triads Example: Bass Line

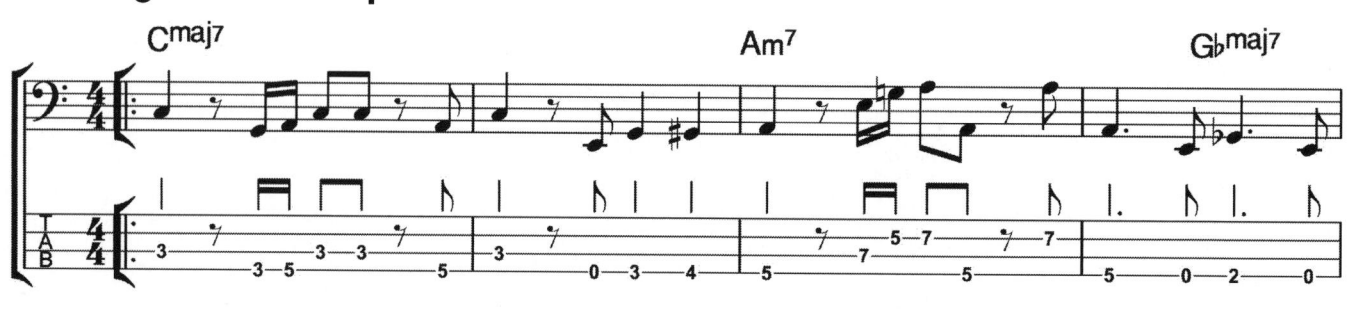

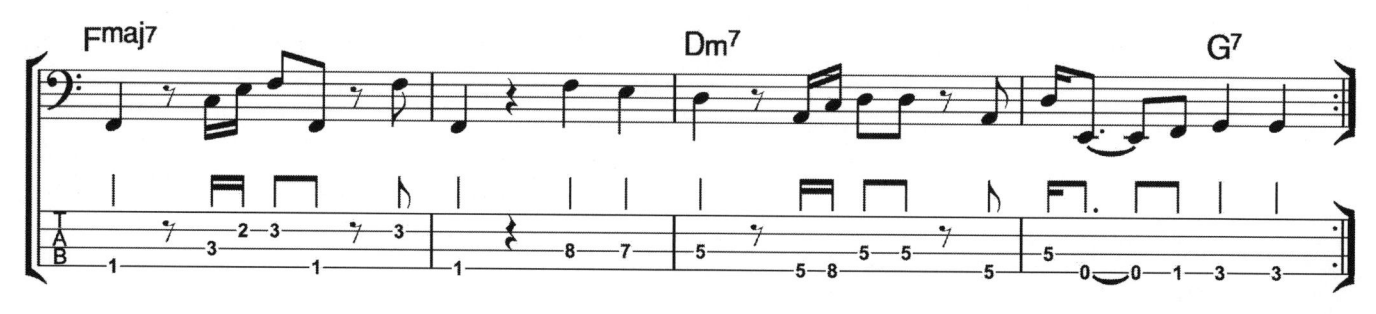

PERFORMANCE

All of the techniques and concepts covered in the "Composition" section of this book can, of course, be used as the basis of any practice session or live performance. To differentiate them, I want you to think of the following performance concepts as starting points, and building blocks of songs that are going to be recorded in one take. Unlike the composition process when you have the luxury of time at home, these live performances are not something you can refine after the fact whilst onstage. In performance, we move into the mindset of having composition components in our muscle memory. These enhance our real-time ability to stay in a flow-state; being aware of the shape of our loop, the arc of the song, and the communication with the audience.

1) Low End

One of the obvious places to start a loop, especially as a bass player, is a solid bass line: either jamming on a static chord, or making a loop several bars-long with a line that has some harmonic rhythm.

If your bass line is the first thing to go into the pedal, be aware that the more layers you add on top of it, the quieter it will become. I find this to actually be a positive thing. If I center my loop around a groove to begin, then layer more sounds on top of it, chances are I might hear a different bass line a few minutes later into the performance. If the initial line is quiet enough, you can easily play a new line over the top, and completely change the feel of the loop. This concept can become quite useful to create variation in something that is inherently static.

Low End Example: Part 1

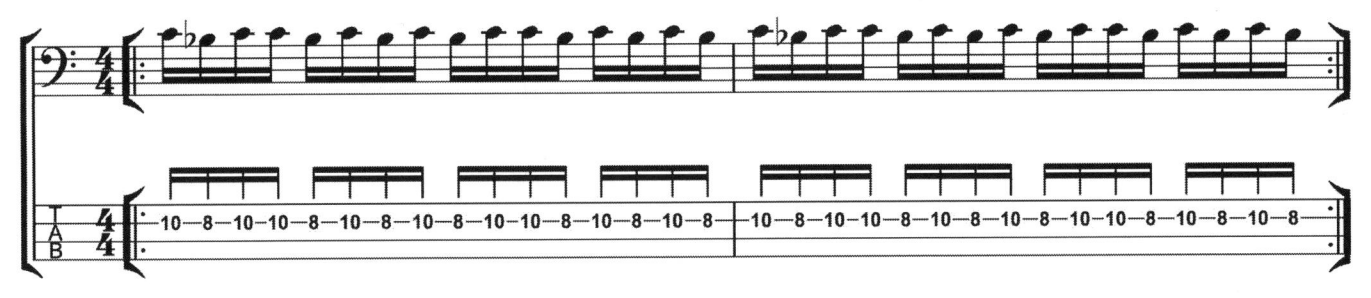

Low End Example: Part 2

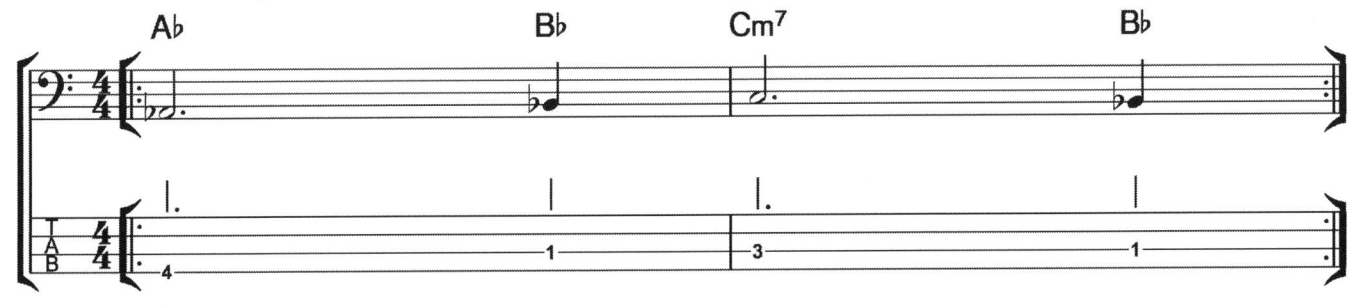

Remember that simple bass lines can have a wide variety of different textures as well. If your initial bass line is clean, then experiment with recording the exact same line again, but adding some sort of modulation or effect on your sound. One of my favorite tools is to play a bass line into the looper with zero effects, and then to track the same thing with an octave pedal—often fattening it up later in the performance, with both the octave and bit crusher pedals together.

Stacking Bass Lines: Low Octave

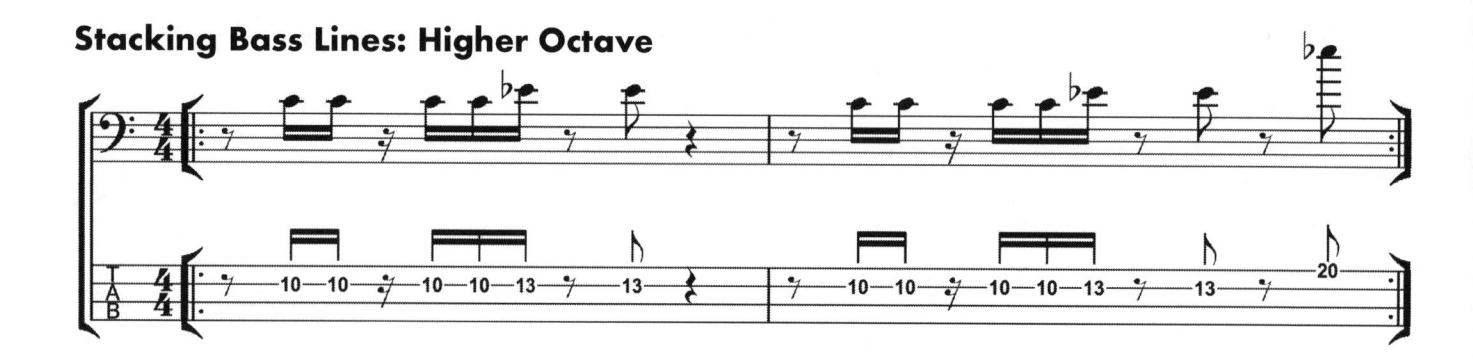

Stacking Bass Lines: Higher Octave

Another important note to keep in mind is how you build the loops up. Be careful not to give away all of the information in the first iteration of the loop—especially when adding bass lines to your groove.

Think about how you would approach jamming over one chord behind a soloist. You would begin with basic ideas, react to what that person is playing, and slowly develop your line as the music grows. Try to manufacture this evolution when you're looping alone, rather than going flat-out the first time you hit the record button.

Slow Builds Example: Part 1

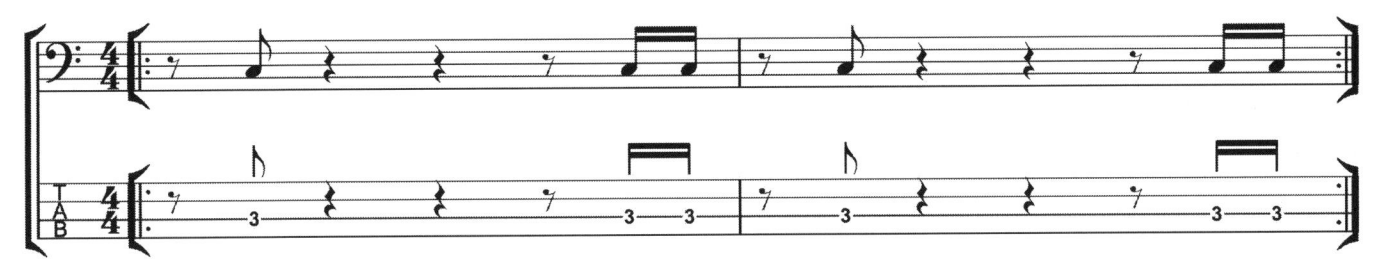

Slow Builds Example: Part 2

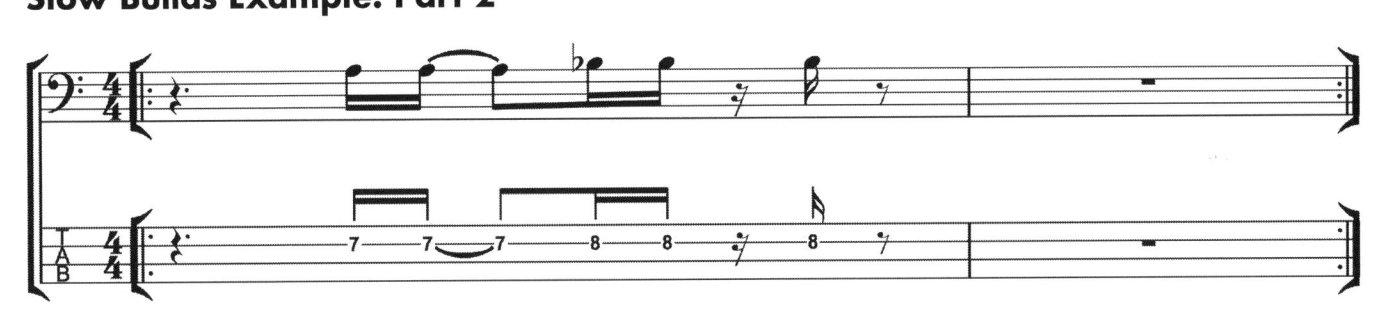

Slow Builds Example: Part 3

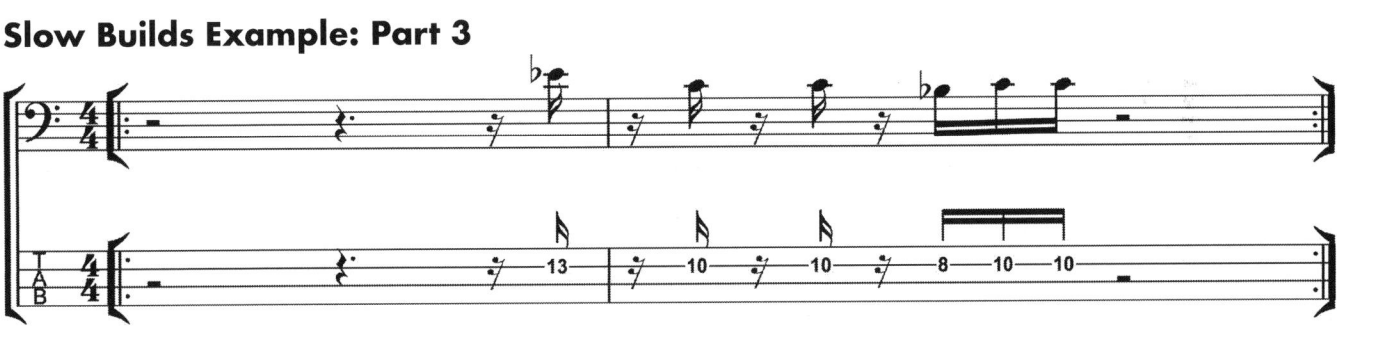

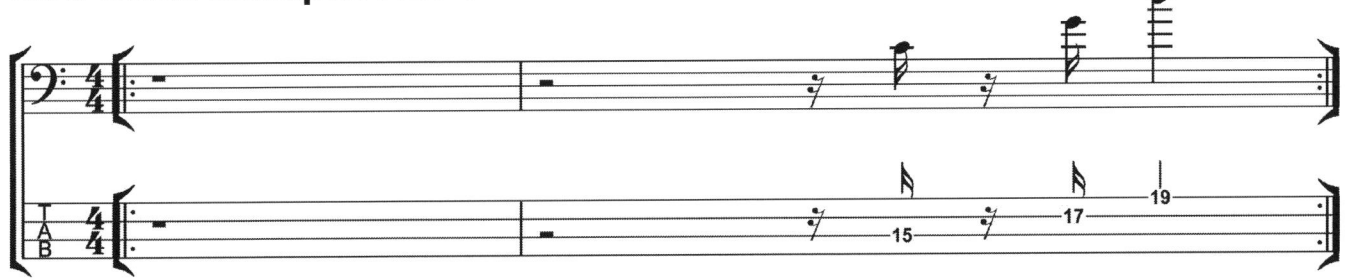

Slow Builds Example: Part 4

In the same spirit of building bass lines over time, remember that you can build question-and-answer segments into your looper using different sounds. I love to put a fat, synth-sounding line into the looper with the Boss OC-2 and the Fredric Effects bit crusher, letting it repeat for a while as I listen for the space. Then I switch off the bit crusher, and play a higher part as an answer to the initial line (with the octave pedal still engaged). You can create an almost programmed or electronic texture with this technique. This same concept of "question and answer" also works without changing sounds at all—just be compositional in the way you build your lines, and don't give away the punchline too soon.

Question & Answer Example: Part 1

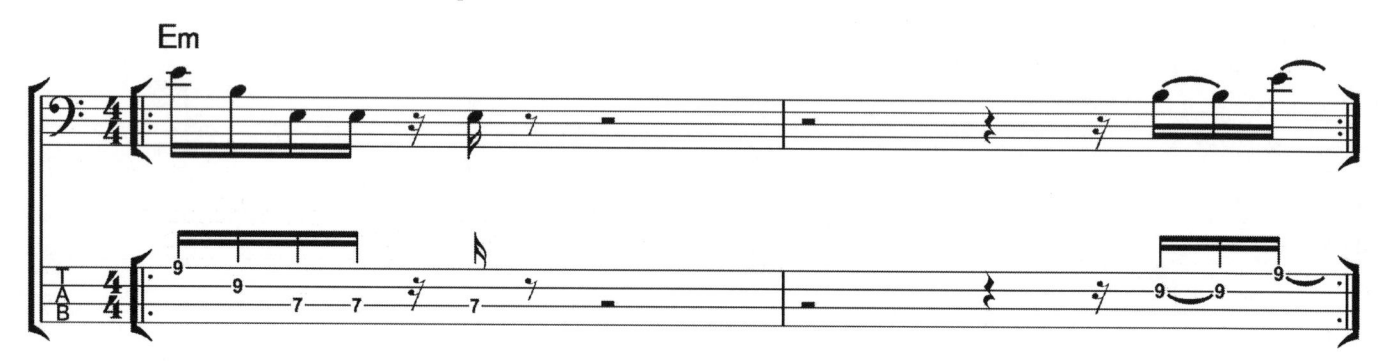

Question & Answer Example: Part 2

Question & Answer Example: Part 3

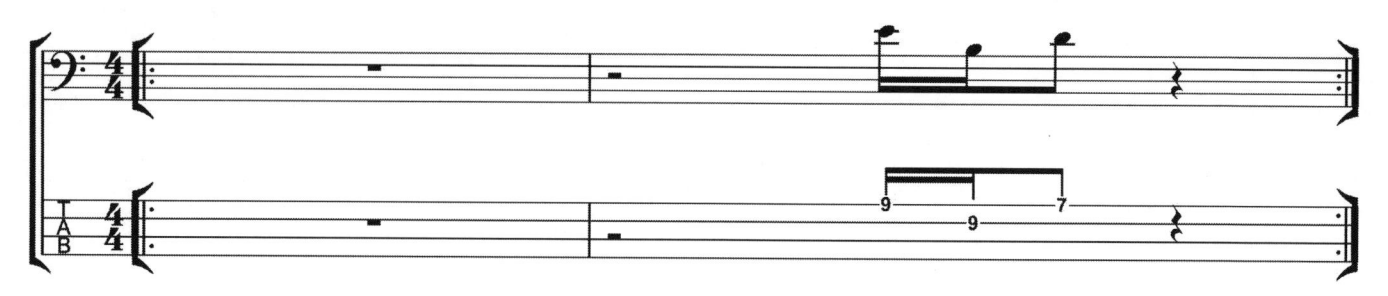

2) High Ostinato (Reharmonization Options)

Approaching the initial loop from the opposite end of the instrument's range can be equally effective as beginning from the low end, and opens up just as many exploratory doors when it comes to reharmonizing your ostinato.

I'm always curious about the third scale degree of the tonality. If I want the largest range of options for harmony underneath the initial ostinanto, I'll avoid locking into a major or minor third right away. I'll either go for a single note, or an interval of a fifth. A single note can obviously go absolutely anywhere, when you think about the concept of any bass note working with any melody note. The interval of a fifth ties you in a little more, but there are still so many interesting sounds to be explored no matter what your initial choice is.

Single Note Ostinato Example

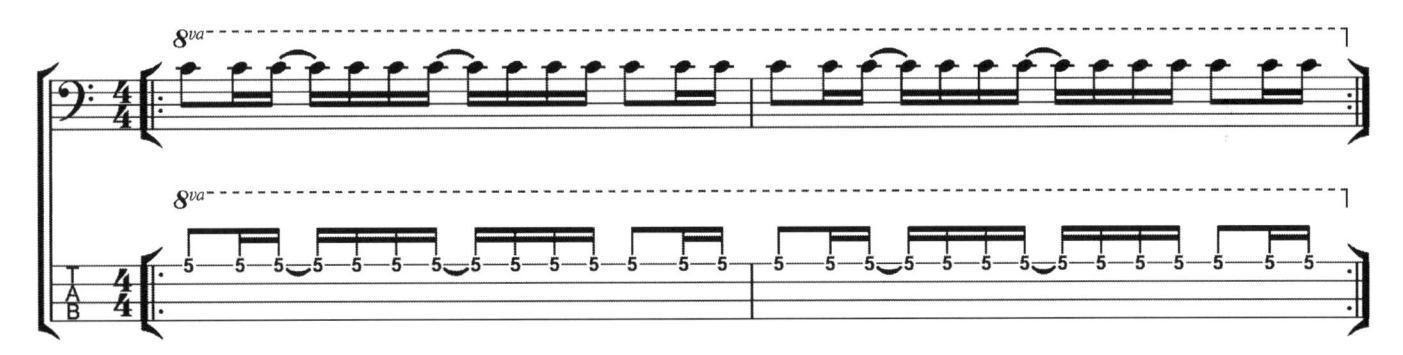

Single Note Ostinato Example: Reharm Option 1

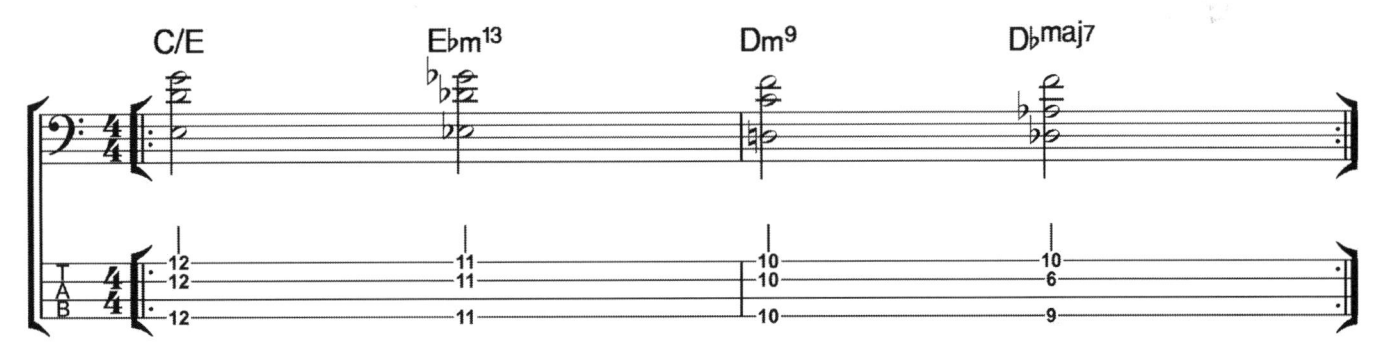

Single Note Ostinato Example: Reharm Option 2

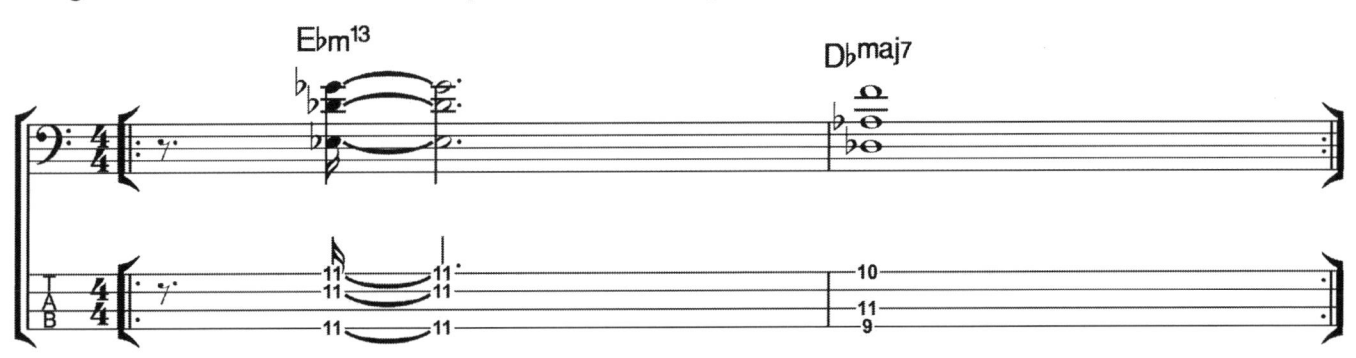

Single Note Ostinato Example: Reharm Option 3

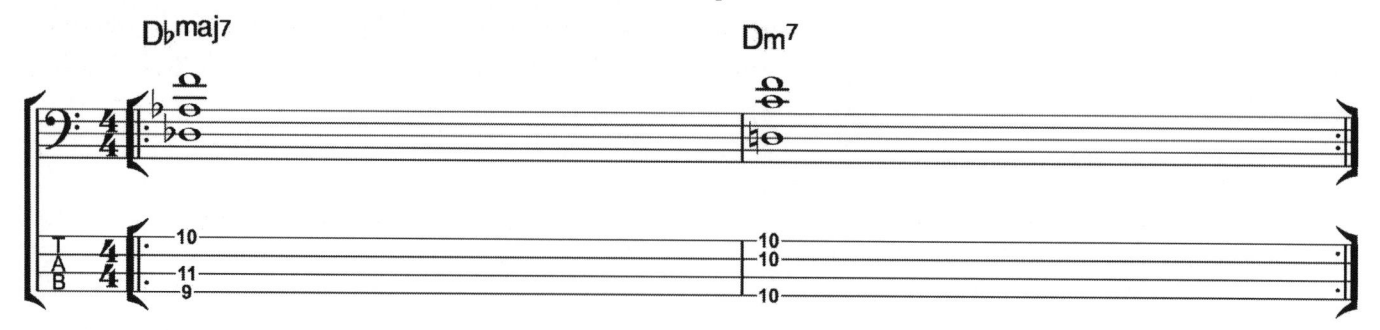

Ostinato with Fifth Example

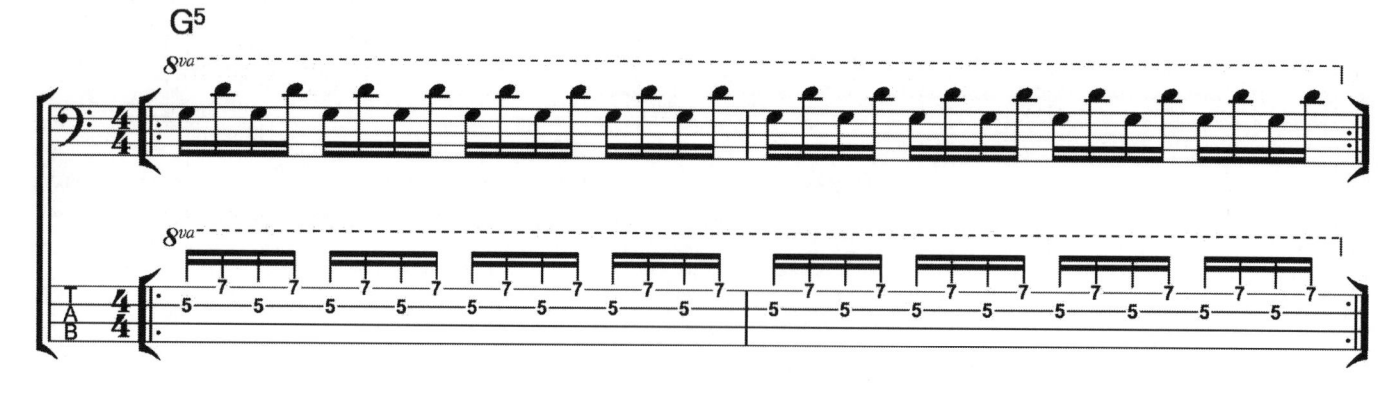

Ostinato with Fifth Example: Reharm Option

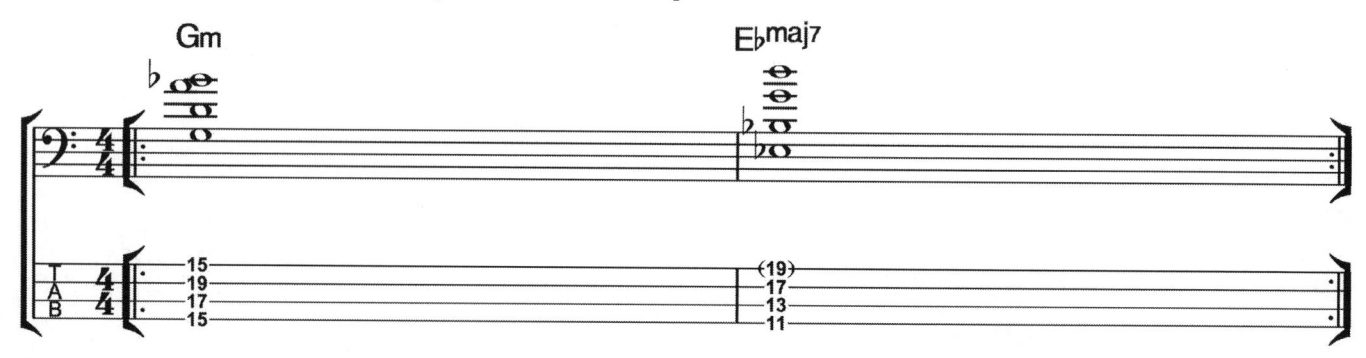

3) Ambient

The basic idea of creating an ambient, rubato landscape can be achieved with just a reverb pedal, and a volume pedal. The idea is to find the range you want to start in, have the volume pedal all the way down (and the volume control on your instrument all the way up), pick the notes you want to sound, and then swell the volume pedal in with reverb on.

This is most effective with a completely washed-out, huge-room setting on your pedal. I love to use the "Church" setting on my TC Electronic Hall of Fame. Almost all reverb pedals will have the option for changing the size of the room they're imitating, as well as knobs to control the mix and the decay of the sound. As you can see from the settings on my pedal, I have both the mix and the decay maxed out, and the room size set to one of the biggest the pedal offers.

You will need to get a feel for what that maxed-out decay feels like, because there's a sweet spot of where it's musical to introduce the next chord change if you're swelling in a sequence of chords. It's easy to go to the next chord too early, and still have the first one ringing too loud. This will result in some pretty gnarly clashes, and doesn't always yield the smoothest results.

Alternately, you might want to stay in one total center and create a huge, cinematic soundscape, which can be very dense and powerful. In this case, experiment with how quickly you can swell each component in—one of top of the other—in order to keep up the intensity of the sound.

Maintaining one tonal center for this drone-like ambient loop makes for really powerful moments when you change the quality of your chord. This can be majorly effective regardless of how huge and dense your soundscape is, or how light and sparse. If we pedal "C" for instance—and don't have a third present, or seventh, or even a fifth for that matter—we can turn that "C" pedal into any tonality we like, because there are no quality-defining notes committed to the recorded loop.

To practice this effect, work on shifting between major and minor at first. While it may seem elementary, I think you'll be amazed at how incredibly different those sounds are when pitted against each other—despite being rooted in the same note.

After these building blocks, of course, the sky is the limit. Any chord quality or slash chord you can think of is fair game.

You can experiment with playing all twelve major triads over a root, for instance. Repeating this exercises over and over is a fantastic tool for your ear, and will give you real-time experience in what each of these tonalities sound like over a static root-note.

There's no substitute for this trial-and-error approach, as you're not restricting yourself to a theory-based, intellectual method of study. You're simply taking a basic component of music—a major triad—and going in search of what that sounds like, regardless of its theoretical harmonic function. Play each of these triads in all three basic inversions (root, first, and second), up and down the neck of the instrument, and then employ that same ambient swelling technique we started the loop with to the triads. You'll discover some amazing performance tools with this exercise.

Triads Over Pedal Drone

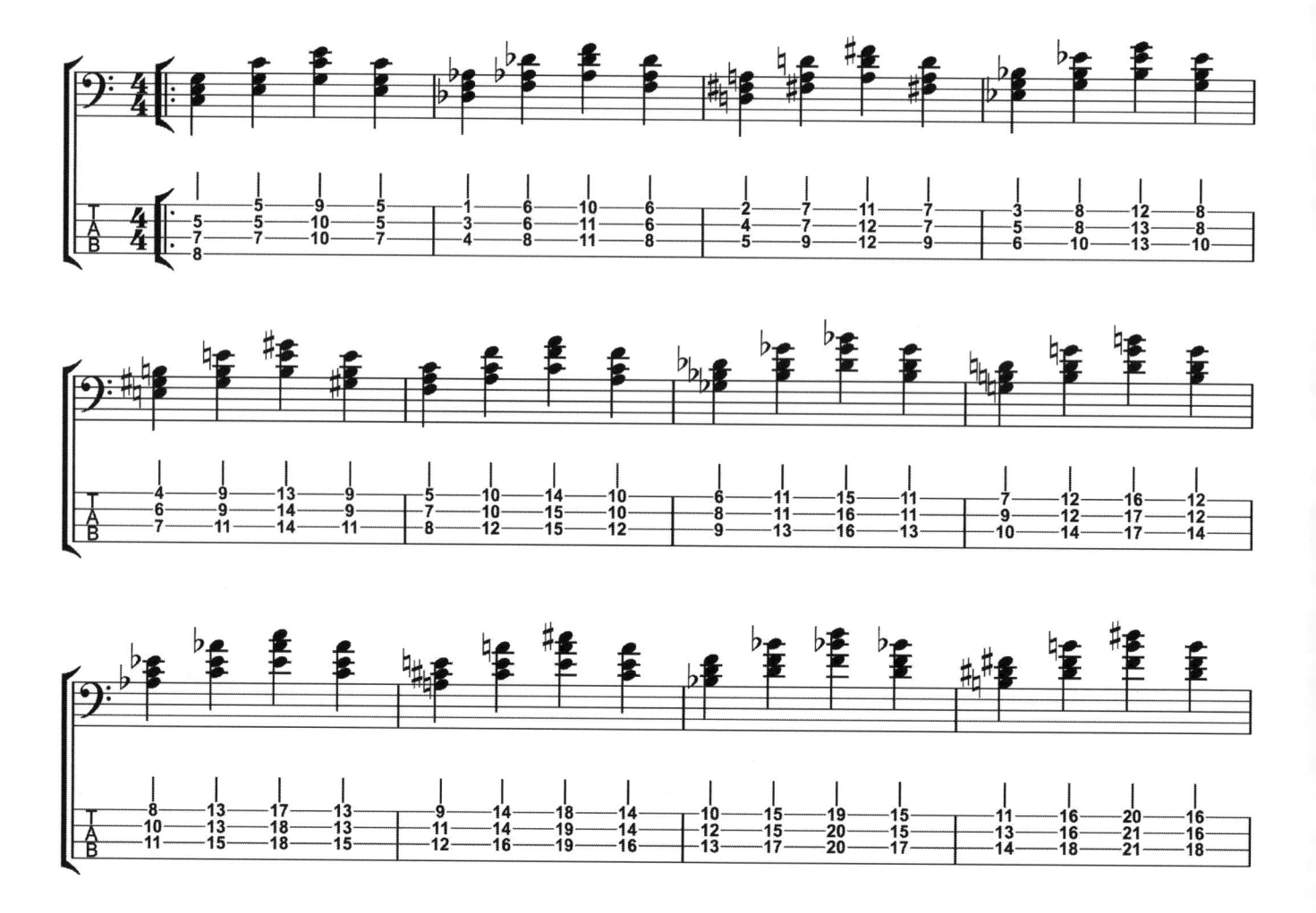

Spread Triads Over Pedal Drone

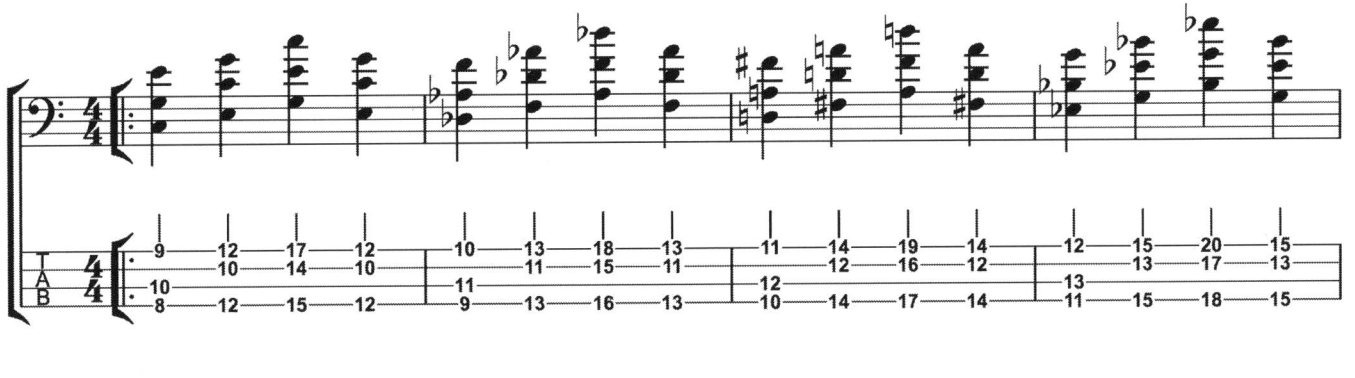

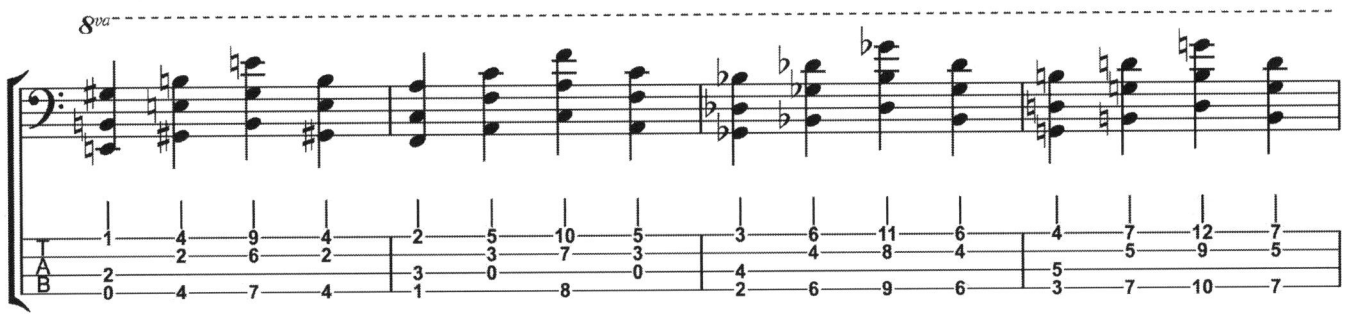

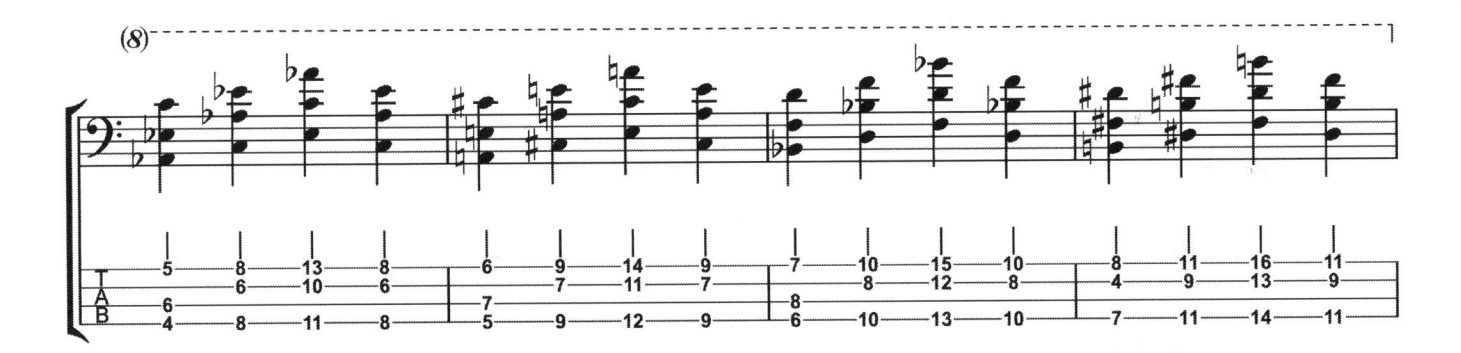

4) Sampling Using a Second Looper

Having two loop pedals on your board can open up an entirely new range of possibilities. With the ambient soundscape we just explored, for example: I'll record into the first looper, and then use the second looper as a sampler to find a tempo from the ambient loop that I can build upon to create a groove. This can turn into a live, improvised composition that might contain melody, groove, percussion, and additional ambient elements.

Although the initial loop is ambient, there is often some rhythmic glitch or hiccup in there that can act as a downbeat on which to build a tempo. And if there isn't, it really doesn't matter! I will literally just find a tempo in my head, and tap that out with my left foot. With the right foot, I'll tap the record button (continuing to monitor the tempo with my left foot). When the required amount of bars have gone by, I'll close the loop, and will now have a downbeat marked—created by the starting point of the new loop.

There will be a clear percussive glitch when sampling an ambient loop, simply by virtue of the fact that you are recording a source that's already in motion. That's not always something you want on a clean loop of a bass line, but in this case it's an awesome byproduct of the inaccurate nature of recording samples this way.

It's really important to keep the tempo locked-in when doing this, and I'm always quick to add a percussive element to solidify the track, making that initial layer rock-solid.

**Mini Ditto Looper:
Secondary/Sampler**

**Ditto X2:
Primary**

Sampling with a Second Looper Example

Another variation on this idea is to play your first percussive element at the same time that you're sampling the ambient loop into the second looper. It does lock you in to the percussion dynamically early-on in the performance, but this technique can make a big difference in that initial layer of the new loop feeling completely air-tight.

5) How Many Layers to Add at Once

Something I've struggled with over the years is how many layers to commit to at one time in a looping performance. A feature of the Ditto looper, and something I believe is becoming more and more common these days, is the "undo" function. By holding down the record button while the loop is playing, it will take away the last thing you recorded; and vise versa, it can also "redo," bringing back the last thing you recorded.

Now the question becomes: how much can you add to your performance, in terms of form and variation, by adding and subtracting large sections of your loop with full control of the "undo" and "redo" functions?

The way I most often implement this feature is by creating dynamic interest in my performance. I will build up my loop with the song form, including groove, chords, and percussion; then state the melody, typically followed by its harmony. I am then able to remove the melody and harmony with the "undo" function, leaving the song form intact to solo over. I then have the option to bring back the melody after the solo, without having to play it again.

A variation on this exercise could be to only state the melody with no harmony notes first; then remove it from the loop, and play a solo; then bring the melody back at the end of the piece, finally adding the harmony notes to build the performance to a climax.

**Left Stomp Button:
"Undo" & "Redo" Functions**

Adding Layers Example: Melody Without Harmony

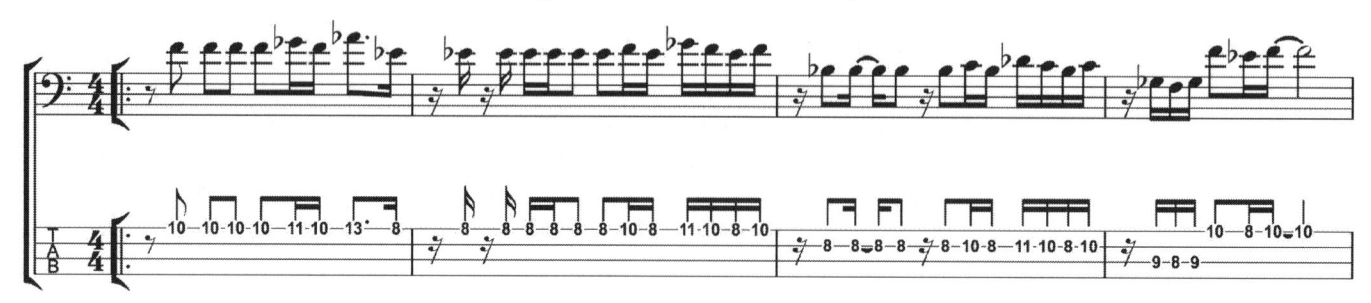

Adding Layers Example: Harmony for Melody

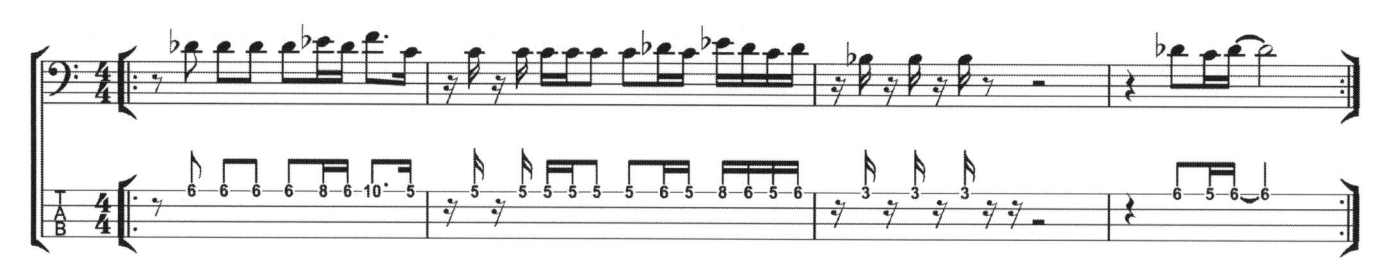

LOOPING WITH A DRUMMER/BAND

1) General Monitoring Tips

There are products on the market right now, such as the TC Electronic Ditto X2 Jam, that have a microphone installed to detect the ebb and flow of your metronomic time. This microphone ensures the loop will always be in time with what's going on around it. Although I haven't personally tried this pedal, the concept seems to be very solid.

For anyone who doesn't have that pedal, I would suggest making sure you have a higher-pitched percussive element for the drummer to use as a click of sorts. Always remember that you can re-add that element if it starts to get lost underneath new components of the loop. I've experimented with this method for many years now, and while it really depends on who the drummer is and how much they understand this unique way of performing, it has served me incredibly well over the years.

I use the Boss PS5 to get those super high-pitched percussive notes, but be careful: if you're caught up in the moment and have perhaps added a clean boost to your signal chain, or have turned up the bass to be heard over the looper, adding those high-pitched percussion parts can really stick out, and not in a good way. I've had a few funny looks from people on the bandstand when I get it wrong, and people's ears don't respond well to a dog-whistle-style pitch suddenly coming out of your amplifier.

2) Mixing the Loop with the Band

One of the things I love about looping in an ensemble situation, with musicians who really listen (which is another massive key to make this successful), is having something harmonic or melodic in the loop for the melodic or comping instruments to latch onto. Once they start to play along with the loop, you can slowly fade out the pedal and go completely live. This is live composition in real-time, and once you hand off the baton to the band and you are no longer locked with that 4-bar loop, there are so many places you can take the idea.

Something I'm very particular about when there are other musicians with me in a live-looping situation is clearly cueing to the band as to when they should get involved. Unless you've been working with the musicians around you for a long time, the chances that they're going to have the same exact vision for the loop that you do are pretty slim. There's nothing worse for me than barely getting started in building my loop, and the drummer is already tinkering away. That can completely break the mood, and immediately eliminates 50% of the dynamic potential you have to build the sonic landscape on your terms.

To counteract this, discussing the performance beforehand is paramount. Let the musicians know roughly where you'd like to get to before they get involved. It shouldn't be ego based, because you don't have a scripted routine that you have to nail every time in a certain sequence. Rather, you want to make the other musicians around you aware of the potential scope of where the performance might go, and for everyone to be patient before joining you—the more patient, the better.

CLOSING THOUGHTS

My hope, now that you're at the end of the book, is that you have a few more concepts to integrate into your routine. Whether you're about to take over the world as a solo artist, or have always wanted more out of your composition or practice-process at home, the ideas in this book should help you make some headway.

I hate to have a feeling of being overwhelmed when I play, and I'm always looking for the most relaxed state possible, with a clear head and an ability to start from zero. With that in mind, I try to have a combination of two or three things in the forefront of my mind before I pick up my instrument. Here are a few examples of those pre-work thoughts that you might like to try for yourself. But remember, everyone is different. Start making notes about things that are important for your process, and create unique lists like this of your own.

Practice:

1. **Listen to your body:** if it's cold, make sure you spend long enough warming up. If there's pain somewhere, allow for the possibility that resting might be more valuable than practicing
2. **Honesty over ego:** You might have an idea that you just know is the hippest thing, and is definitely what you need to practice right away. But let honesty get the better of the ego by playing something simple, and making sure your process isn't hindered in any way.
3. **Is the red light on?** Make sure you are recording you practice at all times. Don't let great ideas get lost because you weren't able to stop in the middle of your flow-state and write them down.

Composition:

1. **Find the form:** I'm always looking to find form in what I do, as that helps make the story of a composition cohesive.
2. **Melody over everything:** Melody is almost always the most important part of what I'm doing. Having this thought in the forefront of my mind as I compose helps serve the music, and not sacrifice composition for selfish, instrument-specific ability.
3. **Go back to the original idea:** It's easy to get a long way from your starting point as you develop ideas. But quite often, if the idea was strong enough to develop in the first place, it's helpful to go back and re-visit the concept in its most basic form to see if that will help tie the entire composition together.

Performance:

1. **Don't be afraid of the audience:** Don't forget, they came to see you. They are on your side. Welcome them in to what you're doing right away to make it a collaborative effort, rather than an internal struggle about what they might be thinking of you.
2. **Pace the show:** We don't have to give it all away immediately. Let the music come to you, let the audience crave more, and learn to feed off of their energy. Get a dialogue going as soon as possible to make them feel like they're a part of what you're doing.
3. **Trust your instincts:** When you have any question as to whether you should play another chorus of a solo, or whether there has been too much repetition and it's time for a change - trust your first instinct. Don't play the extra chorus, and make the change. It's always better to leave people wanting more, than to leave them exhausted from too much information.

ALSO BY
JANEK GWIZDALA

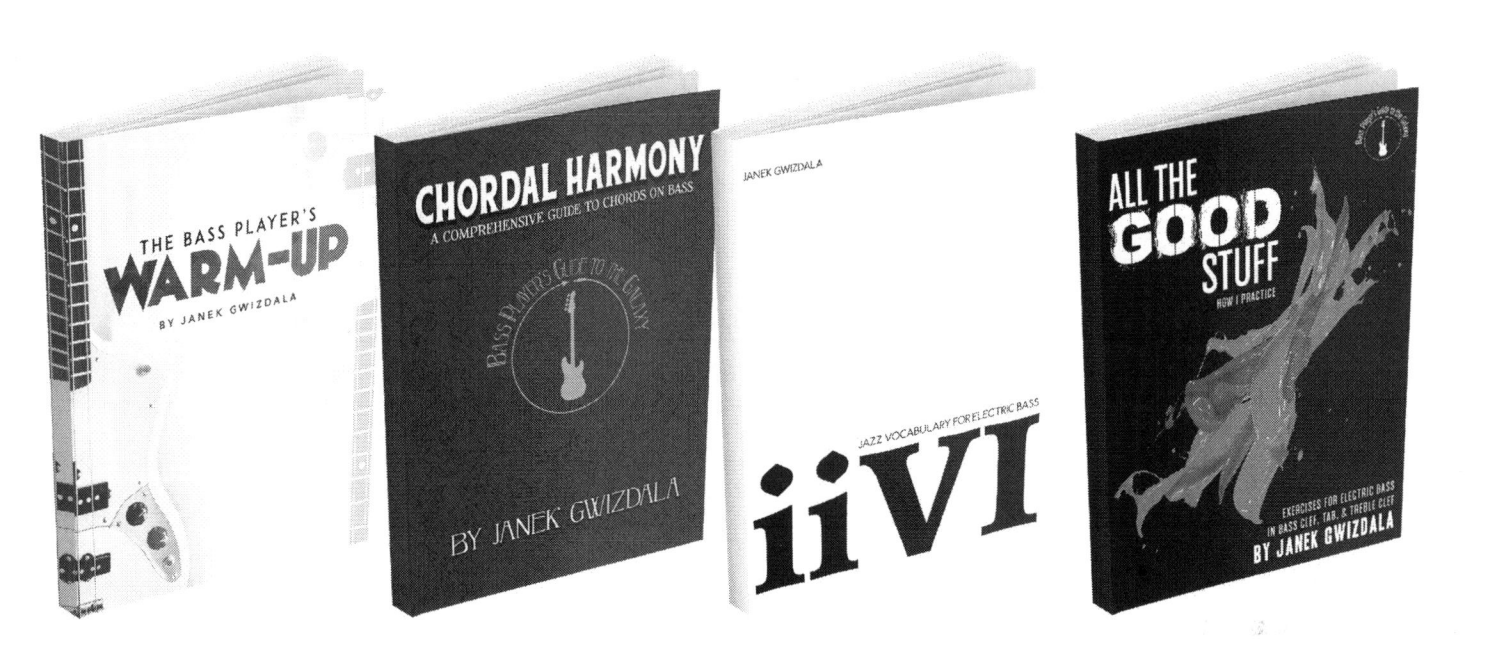

Online Music Lessons:
www.janeksbassstudio.com

YouTube Channel:
youtube.com/janekgwizdala

More Products & Information:
shop.janekgwizdala.com

ABOUT THE AUTHOR

London-born, US-based bass player and record producer **Janek Gwizdala** has been on the international music scene for over twenty years, touring as a band leader and working as musical director or sideman with some of the most respected names in the industry. These include: Randy Brecker, Carlos Santana, Bob Reynolds, Hiram Bullock, Mike Stern, John Mayer, Airto Moreira, Chuck Loeb, Peter Erskine, Flora Purim, Pat Metheny, Billy Cobham, John Patitucci, Bob Mintzer, Marcus Miller, Jojo Mayer, Dennis Chambers, and Wayne Krantz. As a recording artist, Janek has released eleven albums as band leader; as an author, has published twelve critically acclaimed books; and has toured the world extensively as both a musician, and as a lecturer & clinician at the world's leading educational establishments.

Made in the USA
Columbia, SC
09 December 2019

GRADE 2

The Syllabus of Examinat... of requirements, especiall... and sight-reading. Attenti... Special Notices on the fron... is given of changes.

The syllabus is obtainabl... ...ers or from The Associated Board of the Royal Schools of Music, 14 Bedford Square, London WC1B 3JG (please send a stamped addressed C5 envelope).

In centres outside the UK, information may be obtained from the Local Representative.

REQUIREMENTS

SCALES AND ARPEGGIOS (from memory)

Scales
(i) in similar motion, hands together one octave apart, and each hand separately, in the following keys: G, D, A, E, F majors and E, B, D minors (melodic *or* harmonic minor at candidate's choice) (all two octaves)
(ii) in contrary motion, both hands beginning and ending on the key-note (unison), in the keys of C and E majors (two octaves)

Chromatic Scale
each hand separately, beginning on D (one octave)

Arpeggios
the common chords of G, D, A, E and F majors, and E, B and D minors, in root position only, each hand separately (two octaves)

PLAYING AT SIGHT (see current syllabus)

AURAL TESTS (see current syllabus)

THREE PIECES

LIST A *page*
1 **Johann Wilhelm Hässler** (1747–1822)
 Ecossaise in G, No. 23 from
 50 Pieces for Beginners, Op. 38 — 2
2 **Joseph Haydn** (1732–1809)
 Scherzo: Sonata in F, Hob. XVI/9, third movement — 3
3 **Henry Purcell** (1659–1695)
 Hornpipe in B flat, Z. T683 — 4

LIST B
1 **Emil Breslaur** (1836–1899)
 A Romp, Op. 46 No. 32 — 5
2 **Cornelius Gurlitt** (1820–1901)
 Serenade in B flat, No. 18 from
 Album for the Young, Op. 140 — 6
3 **Carl Reinecke** (1824–1910)
 Prelude: Serenade in C, Op. 183 No. 1,
 first movement — 8

LIST C
1 **Béla Bartók** (1881–1945)
 'Romanian Christmas Carol', No. 4 from
 Romanian Christmas Carols, Series 1 — 9
2 **Christopher Norton**
 'Cloudy Day', No. 6 from *Microjazz I* — 10
3 **Michael Rose**
 'Cakes and Ale', from *Finger-Fun* — 12

Candidates must prepare three pieces, one from each of the three Lists, A, B and C. Candidates may choose from the pieces printed in this volume or any other piece listed for the grade. Full lists are given in the syllabus and on the inside covers of the *Selected Piano Examination Pieces, 1999–2000*.

Editor for the Associated Board: **Richard Jones**

© 1998 by The Associated Board of the Royal Schools of Music

No part of this publication may be copied or reproduced in any form or by any means without the prior permission of the publishers.

Music origination by Barnes Music Engraving Ltd.
Printed in Great Britain by Headley Brothers Ltd, The Invicta Press, Ashford, Kent

Where appropriate, pieces have been checked with original source material and edited as necessary for instructional purposes. Fingering, phrasing, pedalling, metronome marks and the editorial realization of ornaments (where given) are for guidance but are not comprehensive or obligatory.

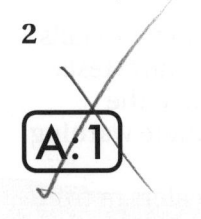

Ecossaise in G

No. 23 from *50 Pieces for Beginners*, Op. 38

Edited by Howard Ferguson

HÄSSLER

Johann Wilhelm Hässler (1747–1822) was a German musician who settled in Russia, where he became influential as a piano teacher. The slurs in bars 9 & 11, R.H., and 10, L.H., are editorial suggestions only.
Source: *Cinquante Pièces à l'usage des commençans*, Op. 38 (Moscow, n.d.).

© 1987 by The Associated Board of the Royal Schools of Music
Reprinted from Hässler, *Fifty Pieces for Beginners*, Op. 38, edited by Howard Ferguson (Associated Board)

Scherzo

Third movement from Sonata in F, Hob. XVI/9

HAYDN

This Scherzo forms the finale of the early Sonata in F, Hob. XVI/9, written before Haydn became Kapellmeister to Prince Nikolaus Esterházy in 1766. Semiquavers should be crisply articulated throughout and repeated quavers *staccato* (H.F.). Dynamics and slurs are editorial suggestions only. For this edition, bar 23 has been assimilated to bar 7, as in Haydn's Piano Trio in C, Hob. XV/39. In the original Scherzo movement, bar 23 is given as

Source: *IV Divertimenti à Clavicembalo Solo del Sigr. Hayden*, Staatsbibliothek zu Berlin, Preussischer Kulturbesitz, Mus. ms. 10116.

© 1998 by The Associated Board of the Royal Schools of Music
Selected from Haydn, *Selected Keyboard Sonatas*, Book I, edited by Howard Ferguson (Associated Board)

Hornpipe in B flat

Z. T683

PURCELL

This lively hornpipe was originally written for strings, forming part of Purcell's incidental music to the play *Abdelazer, or the Moor's Revenge* by Aphra Behn. Unmarked quavers should be *staccato* and L.H. crotchets lightly detached. Dynamics and slurs are editorial suggestions only.
Source: London, The British Library, Add. MS 22099.

© 1998 by The Associated Board of the Royal Schools of Music
Selected from *Baroque Keyboard Pieces*, Book I, edited by Richard Jones (Associated Board)

A Romp
Op. 46 No. 32

Edited by
Lionel Salter

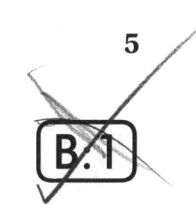

BRESLAUR

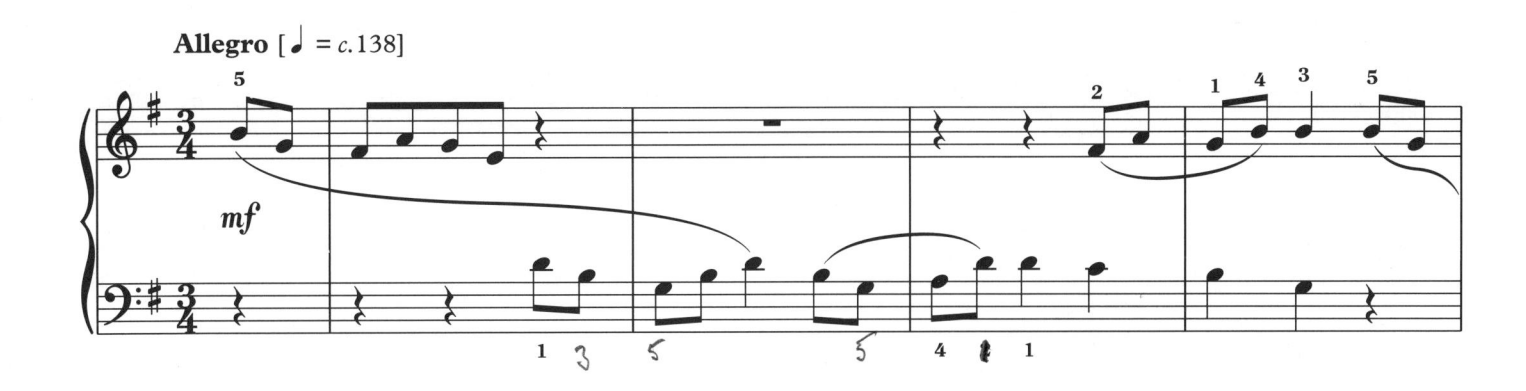

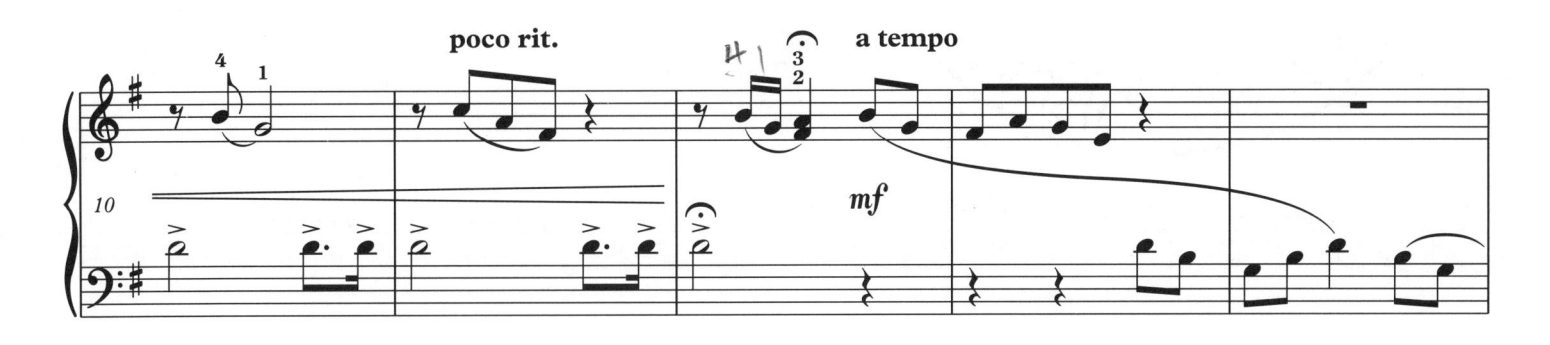

Emil Breslaur's (1836–99) life was a busy one. Besides teaching in Berlin (where he founded a Teachers' Association) and editing a magazine on music education, he was also a synagogue cantor. (L.S.)

© 1986 by The Associated Board of the Royal Schools of Music
Reprinted from *Short Romantic Pieces for Piano*, Book I, edited by Lionel Salter (Associated Board)

Serenade in B flat
No. 18 from *Album for the Young*, Op. 140

GURLITT

Cornelius Gurlitt (1820–1901) was a Danish-born pianist and composer who taught in Copenhagen and Hamburg, and was strongly influenced by Schumann. Much of his piano music was written for teaching purposes. The L.H. accompaniment should be *legato* throughout.
Source: *Album pour la Jeunesse (Jugend-Album)*, Op. 140, London, n.d. (before 1886).

© 1998 by The Associated Board of the Royal Schools of Music
Selected from *A Romantic Sketchbook for Piano*, Book I, edited by Alan Jones (Associated Board)

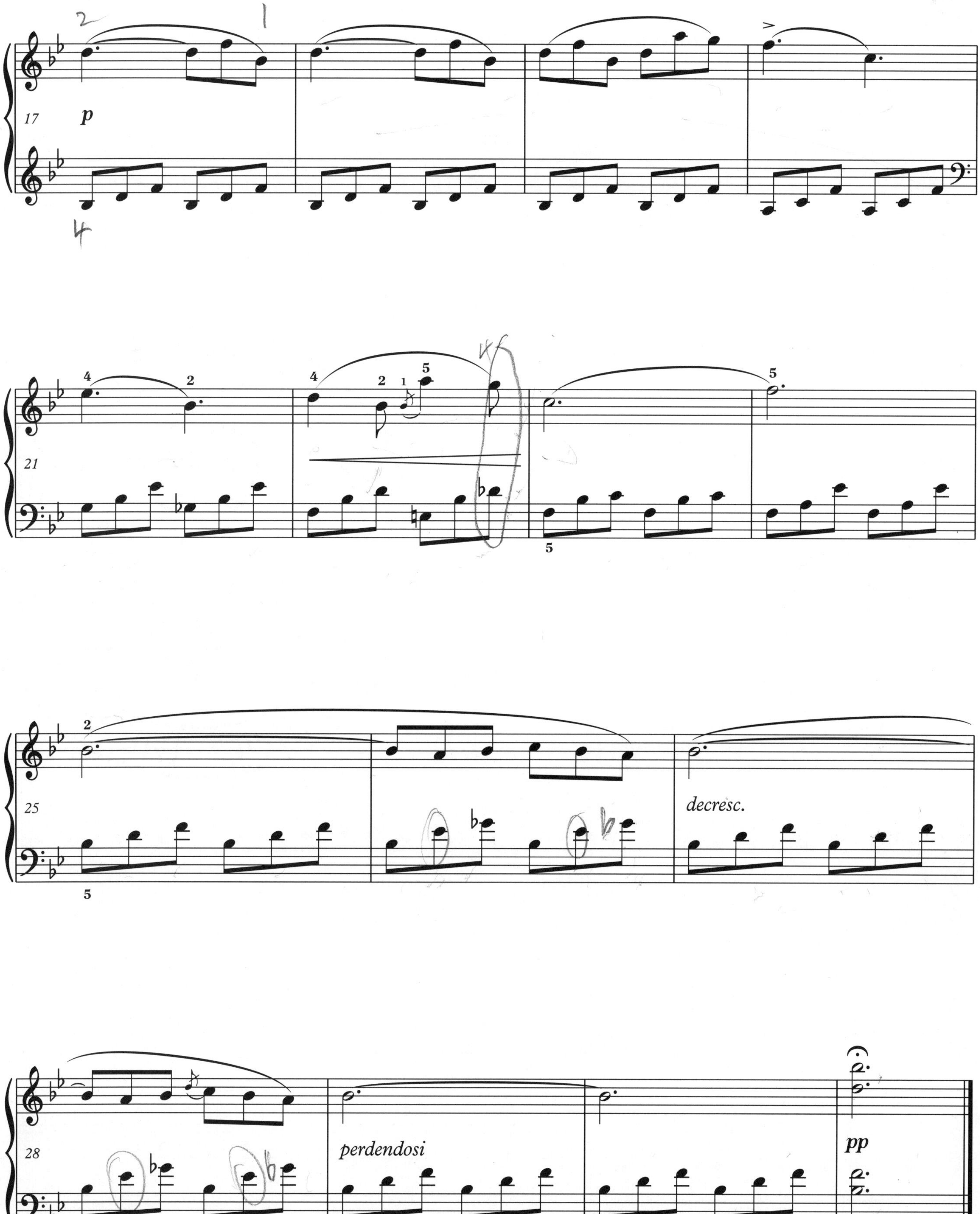
p
decresc.
perdendosi
pp

Prelude

First movement from Serenade in C, Op. 183 No. 1

REINECKE

Carl Reinecke (1824–1910) was a prolific German composer, influenced by Schumann and Mendelssohn, as well as professor of composition at the Leipzig Conservatoire and conductor of the celebrated Leipzig Gewandhaus Orchestra.
Source: *Fünf Clavier-Serenaden für die Jugend*, Op. 183 (Leipzig, 1885).

© 1998 by The Associated Board of the Royal Schools of Music
Selected from Reinecke, *Five Serenades for the Young*, Op. 183, edited by Alan Jones (Associated Board)

Romanian Christmas Carol

No. 4 from *Romanian Christmas Carols*, Series 1

BARTÓK

Cloudy Day

No. 6 from *Microjazz I*

CHRISTOPHER NORTON

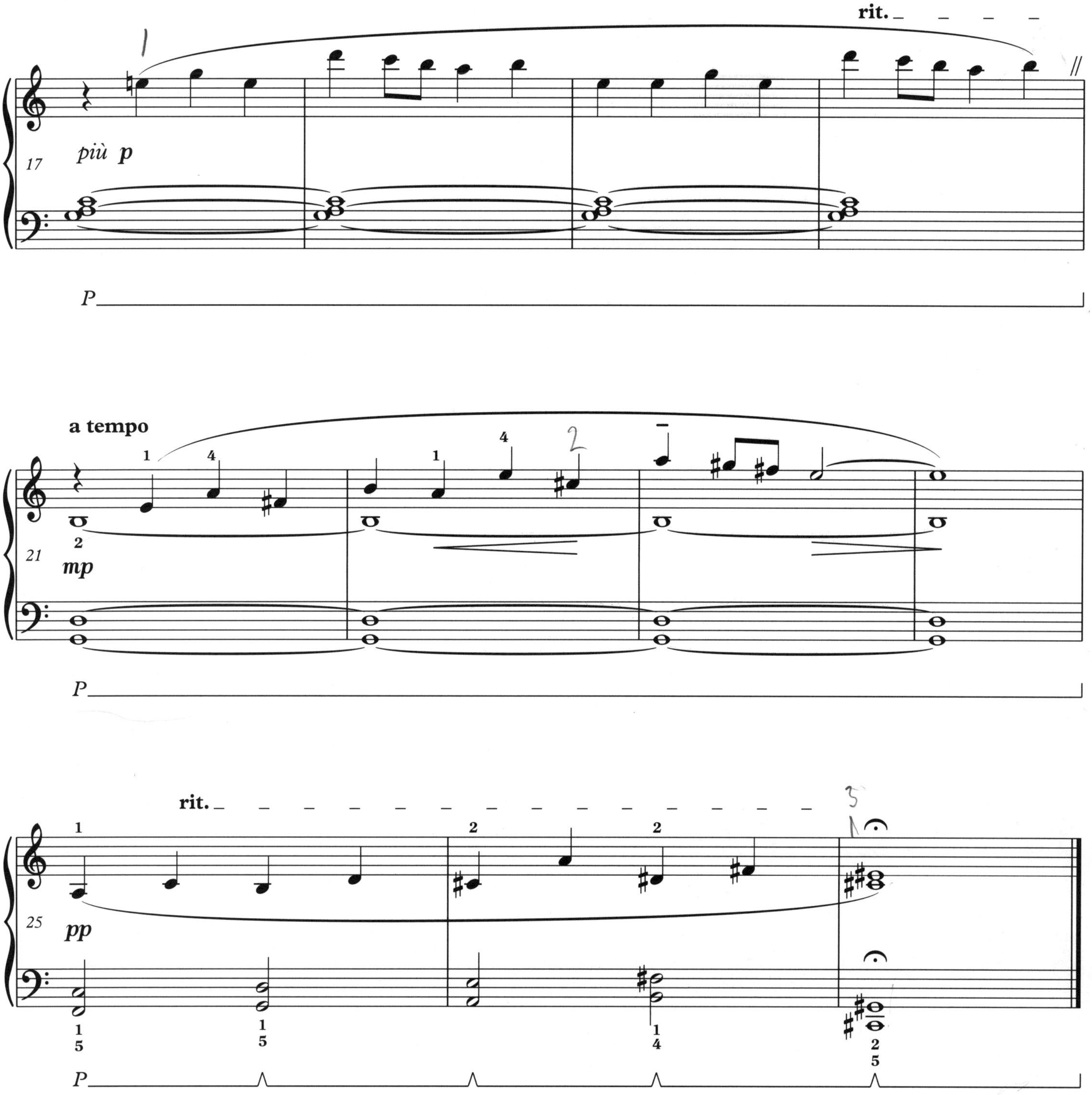
rit.
più p
a tempo
mp
rit.
pp

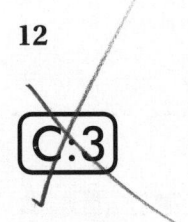

Cakes and Ale

from *Finger-Fun*

MICHAEL ROSE